# MAYER SMITH

*Lunar Claw*

*Copyright © 2025 by Mayer Smith*

*All rights reserved. No part of this publication may be reproduced, stored or transmitted in any form or by any means, electronic, mechanical, photocopying, recording, scanning, or otherwise without written permission from the publisher. It is illegal to copy this book, post it to a website, or distribute it by any other means without permission.*

*This novel is entirely a work of fiction. The names, characters and incidents portrayed in it are the work of the author's imagination. Any resemblance to actual persons, living or dead, events or localities is entirely coincidental.*

*Mayer Smith asserts the moral right to be identified as the author of this work.*

*Mayer Smith has no responsibility for the persistence or accuracy of URLs for external or third-party Internet Websites referred to in this publication and does not guarantee that any content on such Websites is, or will remain, accurate or appropriate.*

*Designations used by companies to distinguish their products are often claimed as trademarks. All brand names and product names used in this book and on its cover are trade names, service marks, trademarks and registered trademarks of their respective owners. The publishers and the book are not associated with any product or vendor mentioned in this book. None of the companies referenced within the book have endorsed the book.*

*First edition*

*This book was professionally typeset on Reedsy.*
*Find out more at reedsy.com*

# Contents

| | | |
|---|---|---|
| 1 | The Call of the Moon | 1 |
| 2 | Unveiling the Past | 7 |
| 3 | The Shadow's Edge | 13 |
| 4 | Whispers of Betrayal | 20 |
| 5 | The Hunt Begins | 27 |
| 6 | Tides of the Moon | 34 |
| 7 | Through the Fire | 41 |
| 8 | The Witch's Secret | 48 |
| 9 | The Hidden City | 56 |
| 10 | Echoes of War | 63 |
| 11 | Bloodlines Converge | 70 |
| 12 | The Wolf Within | 77 |
| 13 | The Thieves' Gambit | 84 |
| 14 | The Forbidden Rite | 91 |
| 15 | Betrayal at Dusk | 98 |
| 16 | The Gathering Storm | 105 |
| 17 | Blood Moon Rising | 112 |
| 18 | The Heart of Darkness | 118 |
| 19 | The Last Shifter | 124 |
| 20 | Into the Abyss | 131 |
| 21 | The Final Trial | 138 |
| 22 | The Shifting Tide | 145 |
| 23 | The War Within | 152 |
| 24 | Unity or Ruin | 158 |

25 The Legacy of the Claw 164

**One**

# The Call of the Moon

S cene: A dimly lit room, the shadows of tall, twisting trees cast across the stone walls through a small, circular window. The wind howls outside, carrying with it the scent of pine and rain. A lone figure, KIAN, a young wolf shifter, stands at the edge of a wooden table, his brow furrowed in concentration as he pores over an ancient tome. His breathing is heavy, the weight of the prophecy he is studying almost unbearable. The silence of the room is broken only by the distant echo of wolves howling in the forest beyond.

Kian: (muttering to himself)
"'The Claw, the Claw… unite or destroy.' How can such power lie in the hands of one? Who would dare…"

(He pauses, his eyes flicking over the pages, his fingers tracing the cryptic symbols. His heartbeat quickens.)

Kian: (in a low voice, almost to himself)
"Could it really be true? The Lunar Claw? Is it… really waiting for me?"

(He slams the book shut, frustrated. The room seems to pulse with a strange energy. The howling grows louder, closer now.)

Voice in the Dark: (a deep, gravelly voice, echoing from the shadows)
"You should not be reading that, Kian."

(Kian spins around, his wolf senses on alert. Standing in the doorway is SEVERIN, an elder of the clan, his face hidden beneath the hood of a dark cloak. His eyes gleam with an unsettling knowledge, as if he has seen things no one should ever see.)

Kian: (startled, his voice shaking)
"Severin… how did you—"

Severin: (stepping into the room, his voice calm but firm)
"The Claw is no mere legend, Kian. It is not a thing for the young, the restless, the unprepared. It calls to you, yes, but it is a dangerous thing to answer."

(Severin walks slowly toward the table, his eyes never leaving Kian's. He places a weathered hand on the book, pushing it aside with surprising strength.)

## The Call of the Moon

Severin: (sighs, almost pityingly)
"I had hoped you would never come across it. But I see now that fate is a thing of its own design. And your path is already set."

Kian: (defensive, his hands clenching into fists)
"Why do you speak as if you know me? What is this 'Claw' really? You say it's dangerous, but you don't tell me why."

Severin: (with a dry laugh, his voice full of years of sorrow)
"Because, boy, the Claw does not belong to you. It belongs to the moon itself. It is an artifact forged by the ancients to unite or destroy. The moon decides what it shall be—"

Kian: (cutting him off, frustrated and incredulous)
"Then why do you speak of it like it's some kind of weapon? You make it sound like something evil—"

Severin: (his tone suddenly dark, his voice low and grave)
"Because it is. But it is also the only hope for the clans. The Claw has the power to reshape our world. To call forth the moon's true power. To unite our fractured tribes under one banner... or shatter everything we have built."

(A long silence hangs between them. Kian struggles to digest the weight of Severin's words.)

Kian: (softly, almost as if in disbelief)
"So, it's true? The clans... they will fight for it?"

Severin: (his eyes narrowing, a grim smile curling on his lips)

"Not just fight, boy. They will kill for it. Your very existence makes you a target. The Claw… it wants to choose a leader, and the moon will choose a worthy heir. And that heir could be you, Kian."

(Kian recoils slightly, his heart racing.)

Kian: (with growing panic)
"Me? Why me? I'm just a wolf—"

Severin: (interrupting, his voice sharp)
"You are more than that. You are the blood of the first clan, the ones who forged the Claw. It calls to you, just as it has called to others before you. But beware—there is darkness in your bloodline, Kian. There is power, yes, but also destruction."

(Kian steps back, his mind spinning.)

Kian: (confused, fearful)
"But what if I don't want this? What if I don't want any part of it?"

Severin: (his gaze softens, but only slightly)
"You have no choice. You were born for this, whether you accept it or not. The Claw will come for you, and when it does, you will either rise with it or fall beneath its weight."

(The howling from outside grows louder still, almost deafening. The wind howls, rattling the windows. Kian feels a sudden, inexplicable chill, as if the very air around him is alive with something ancient and hungry.)

## The Call of the Moon

Kian: (voice trembling)
"Then what should I do? How can I stop it?"

Severin: (his face darkens, his voice lower now)
"You must find it before they do. The rogue clans. The ones who have already begun the hunt. They know about the Claw, and they will stop at nothing to take it for themselves."

(Kian stares at him, his heart pounding in his chest. The weight of the words seems to settle over him like a shroud.)

Kian: (his voice barely a whisper)
"How do I stop them? How do I stop this war?"

Severin: (leaning in close, his voice like a whisper from the grave)
"You don't. You can only prevent the worst from happening. The Claw must never fall into the wrong hands. If it does, the clans will fall into chaos, into ruin. Worse, it could bring about the extinction of the shifters."

(Kian's hands tremble as he reaches for the book again, his eyes burning with a new resolve. He knows, deep down, that he cannot turn away. The Claw is calling him, and no matter how much he fears it, he must answer.)

Kian: (gripping the book, his voice steady but filled with uncertainty)
"Where do I begin?"

Severin: (leaning in closer, his voice low but urgent)

"You will begin at the Temple of the Moon. It is there that the first clue lies. But be warned, Kian, the path will not be easy. There are forces much older and more dangerous than you can imagine already at play."

(Severin turns, his cloak swirling as he begins to leave, his voice carrying one last warning.)

Severin: (from the door, his voice fading into the shadows)
"Do not fail. The moon's call is not one to be ignored… and it will not wait for you forever."

(The door slams shut behind Severin, and Kian is left alone in the dim light, the weight of his destiny pressing down on him. He looks out the small window, the full moon hanging low in the sky, its pale light casting eerie shadows on the ground below.)

Kian: (to himself, a final whisper as he looks up at the moon)
"The Claw… it's coming for me. And I must find it before it's too late."

(The camera zooms in on Kian's face, a mixture of fear and determination in his eyes, as the howling of the wolves grows louder in the distance, echoing through the night. The screen fades to black.)

## Two

# *Unveiling the Past*

Scene: A quiet, secluded forest glade, bathed in the soft, silver light of the full moon. The trees around the glade are ancient, their bark gnarled and thick, as though they've stood sentinel over secrets for centuries. A stone altar sits at the center of the clearing, worn by time but still imposing. The air is thick with tension as KIAN, the young wolf shifter, stands in the center, his body tense with anticipation. He stares at the altar, knowing this place holds the key to everything—the answers he so desperately seeks about the Lunar Claw.

Kian: (whispering to himself, his voice shaky)
"So this is it... the Temple of the Moon. It's just as Severin said. The first clue... it has to be here."

(His footsteps crunch softly on the dry leaves as he moves closer to the altar. His breath catches in his throat as a soft, ancient whisper brushes against his ears, the wind stirring the trees above him.)

Voice in the Wind: (a haunting, feminine voice, barely audible)
"Do not fear, child. The past is not as it seems."

(Kian freezes, his pulse quickening. He glances around, but the forest is still. The whispering voice lingers, almost ethereal, like it's coming from the very air around him.)

Kian: (quietly, almost too afraid to speak)
"Who's there? Show yourself!"

(The wind picks up, swirling around him. The ground beneath his feet seems to hum with an ancient energy. The trees tremble as if the forest itself is watching him. He takes a deep breath, trying to steady his nerves, and steps closer to the altar. The soft glow of moonlight reflects off the stone, revealing intricate carvings—symbols that he has seen before in the ancient book.)

Kian: (whispering, tracing the symbols with his fingers)
"These markings... I've seen them. But where? Why do they feel so familiar?"

(As he traces the carvings, a sudden flash of light erupts from the altar, blinding him momentarily. Kian stumbles back, his heart racing. When the light fades, standing before him is a figure—a woman, ethereal and translucent, her form radiating an otherworldly glow. Her eyes are ancient, yet filled with deep

## Unveiling the Past

sorrow and wisdom. She is dressed in a flowing robe, her long hair moving as if caught in an unseen breeze.)

Woman: (her voice calm, but filled with power)
"You seek the truth, Kian. But do you understand the cost of uncovering it?"

Kian: (stumbling backward, his eyes wide with disbelief)
"Wh—who are you? What is this place? What do you want from me?"

(The woman steps forward, her feet not quite touching the ground, her presence both comforting and unsettling. Her gaze locks with Kian's, and for a moment, it feels as though she can see into his very soul.)

Woman: (her voice soft, as though remembering something long forgotten)
"I am the Guardian of the Claw. The one chosen to watch over the secrets of the past, so that the future might not fall to ruin. But the time has come for the truth to be revealed, Kian. The truth of your lineage."

(Kian's heart skips a beat. He opens his mouth to speak but finds his voice caught in his throat. The woman raises a hand, her fingers glowing with a soft light. Slowly, images begin to appear in the air around them—visions of the past, long-forgotten battles, and the birth of the Claw.)

Woman: (continuing, her tone serious and heavy)
"Your ancestors forged the Lunar Claw, Kian. They were the

ones who bound its power to the moon, and they paid a great price. The Claw was never meant to be wielded by a single ruler—it was meant to unite the clans. But greed… and the thirst for power… corrupted that purpose."

(The images around them shift, showing the first clan leader, a fierce warrior, wielding the Claw in battle. The moon shines brightly overhead, its light illuminating the battlefield.)

Woman: (as the image shifts to darkness)
"Once, there was peace. The Claw united the clans, but soon, factions formed. Those who craved the Claw's power betrayed each other, and the blood of innocents stained the earth. The Claw became a weapon of destruction. The moon withdrew its blessing, and the Claw was hidden. Sealed away, forgotten by all—until now."

(The visions fade, and Kian is left standing in the center of the glade, his mind reeling from the weight of the revelation. The woman's voice echoes in his ears as the vision fades completely.)

Woman: (gently, yet sternly)
"You are the descendant of the bloodline that forged the Claw, Kian. It is your fate to either restore the balance or destroy it once more. The choice is yours, but know this—the Claw does not forgive those who wield it without understanding its true nature."

(Kian stumbles back, trying to make sense of what he's just seen and heard. His mind is a whirlwind of questions. The Claw, his bloodline, the truth—none of it makes sense. But one thing is clear: the fate of the clans is intertwined with his own.)

Kian: (breathing heavily, voice cracking with disbelief)
"But… how? How do I restore balance? How do I stop what has already begun?"

(The woman's eyes soften, her expression full of sorrow.)

Woman:
"You will find the answers in the place where it all began—the Heart of the Moon. It is there that the final truth lies, where the power of the Claw can either be sealed forever or set free to either heal or destroy. But you must hurry, Kian. The rogue clans have already begun their search, and they will stop at nothing to find it before you do."

(Kian's heart skips a beat. He looks down at the ground, feeling the weight of the woman's words settle into his chest like a stone.)

Kian: (quietly, almost to himself)
"The Heart of the Moon… I don't even know where to begin."

Woman: (smiling faintly, her voice now almost a whisper)
"Then listen closely, Kian. The Heart lies beyond the boundaries of your world, in a place few dare to go. Only those pure of heart can find it. The moon will guide you, but you must trust its light, even when darkness threatens to consume you."

(The figure begins to fade, her form dissipating into the wind as the moonlight grows brighter around Kian. Her final words echo in his ears.)

Woman: (her voice soft but urgent)
"Trust the moon, Kian. And remember—every choice you make will shape the future. Choose wisely."

(Kian stands alone in the clearing, his heart heavy with the weight of the prophecy. The wind calms, the air stilling around him. He turns slowly toward the trees, the path ahead uncertain. The Claw, the rogue clans, the Heart of the Moon—everything is suddenly so much bigger than him, and yet somehow, it all leads back to his own bloodline.)

Kian: (to himself, his voice full of resolve)
"I will find the Heart of the Moon. And I will make sure the Claw does not fall into the wrong hands."

(As he steps away from the altar, the full moon above seems to watch over him, its light steady and unyielding. The journey ahead is perilous, but Kian knows one thing for sure: the time for hesitation has passed. The fate of the clans, the legacy of his ancestors, and the future of the world rest on his shoulders.)

(The camera lingers on Kian's face, his expression a mix of fear and determination, before slowly pulling away to reveal the vast, darkened forest that stretches endlessly before him. The wind picks up again, the distant howls of wolves echoing in the night, as if the very forest itself is alive with the call of destiny.)

**Three**

# *The Shadow's Edge*

Scene: A craggy mountain range, the jagged peaks reaching into the sky like the teeth of a great beast. The wind howls, biting and cold, as it sweeps across the barren landscape. Dark clouds churn overhead, casting the area in an oppressive shadow. At the foot of the mountains lies a narrow, winding path, overgrown with thorns and brambles. KIAN, the young wolf shifter, walks steadily along the path, his expression set in determination, but his steps falter every now and then. The weight of his mission presses heavily on him. The Heart of the Moon—he has to find it. But the journey is taking its toll, and every rustling branch, every shifting shadow feels like a threat waiting to strike. As Kian moves forward, the air around him feels thicker, heavier, as though something dark and unseen is watching him, waiting. The hairs on the back of his neck stand on end. His senses are on high alert, the primal instincts of his wolf form urging him to turn back.

But he knows he cannot. Not now. Not when everything is at stake.


Kian: (muttering to himself, voice low and uneasy)
   "Just keep moving. The Heart of the Moon is close. I can feel it. But why does it feel like something's... following me?"

(He pauses for a moment, looking around the bleak landscape. The shadows between the trees stretch unnaturally long, as if reaching out toward him. The wind whips around him, carrying the scent of damp earth and something else—something foreign, something wrong.)

Kian: (narrowing his eyes, suspicious)
   "Is it the wind... or something else?"

(A distant howl echoes across the mountains, carried on the wind. It's not the cry of a wolf—a familiar, distant sound that Kian knows all too well. No, this howl is different. It's too low, too guttural. It vibrates in his chest, sending a chill down his spine.)

Kian: (under his breath, almost to himself)
   "That's not... that's not a wolf."

(He grips the hilt of his dagger, his senses alert as he scans the surrounding area. The howling grows louder, more frantic. And then, as suddenly as it started, it stops. Silence. An eerie, suffocating silence.)

Kian: (whispering to himself, his voice tense)
   "What the hell was that?"

(He begins to move again, more cautiously now, his steps quickening. But as he walks, the shadows seem to lengthen, twisting in ways that don't seem natural. The path ahead becomes darker, the air growing colder with every step. A low growl vibrates in the back of his throat—instinct, urging him to shift, to let his wolf form take control. But he resists. He knows that if he shifts now, he risks giving away his position to whatever lurks in the darkness.)

(A rustling sound breaks the silence. A shadow flits at the corner of his vision—too fast, too fleeting to catch. Kian stops dead in his tracks, every muscle tensed, every sense sharpened. His eyes dart around the clearing, trying to pinpoint the source. The wind picks up, carrying with it the scent of something unnatural, something wrong. His heart pounds in his chest as the rustling grows louder, closer.)

Kian: (whispering urgently, his voice tight)
   "Show yourself."

(The rustling stops abruptly. Then, from the darkness, a figure steps into view—a man, tall and cloaked in black, his face obscured by a hood. He moves with unnatural grace, his presence sending a shiver down Kian's spine. The man's eyes gleam, a piercing silver that reflects the moonlight. There's a coldness to him, an emptiness that makes Kian's gut twist.)

Mysterious Figure: (his voice smooth, almost mocking)

"Don't be afraid, wolf. You've come a long way. But this is where your journey ends."

(Kian takes a step back, his hand instinctively tightening on the dagger's hilt. The man's eyes never leave him, his posture relaxed, almost casual. But Kian senses the danger—every instinct in him screams that this man is no ordinary foe.)

Kian: (keeping his voice steady, though his body is taut with tension)
"Who are you? What do you want?"

Mysterious Figure: (smiling faintly, his voice like a cold wind)
"I am known by many names. But tonight, you may call me the Shadow. And I have been sent to stop you from reaching the Heart of the Moon."

Kian: (his eyes narrowing, heart racing)
"Sent by whom?"

Shadow: (the smile fades, his tone turning dark and serious)
"Does it matter? The ones who sent me are beyond your comprehension. You are a mere pawn in a game far older than you know."

(Kian's grip on his dagger tightens, but he remains silent, trying to read the man's intentions. He knows that any wrong move could be his last.)

Kian: (calmly, keeping his voice low)
"I won't let you stop me. I have to reach the Heart."

Shadow: (laughs softly, as if Kian's defiance amuses him)
  "You misunderstand, boy. I am not here to kill you. Not yet. I am here to warn you."

(Kian tenses, his instincts on high alert.)

Kian: (gritting his teeth)
  "A warning?"

Shadow: (his voice lowering, his eyes flashing with cold fire)
  "Yes. You seek the Heart of the Moon, but you have no idea what you're truly searching for. The Claw… the Heart… they are not what you think. If you continue on this path, you will destroy everything you hold dear."

(Kian's eyes widen, his breath catching. He's heard rumors, whispers of a dark force tied to the Claw, but he never truly believed them. Now, standing face to face with this mysterious figure, the words seem to take on a weight of their own.)

Kian: (voice shaking, unsure)
  "Why are you telling me this? What do you want from me?"

Shadow: (leaning forward slightly, his voice almost a whisper)
  "Because your fate is tied to something much greater than the Claw. You are not merely a wolf shifter, Kian. You are the key. The last piece in a puzzle that will either restore balance or plunge the world into darkness."

(Kian's mind reels. The Shadow's words seem like riddles, but there's a truth to them that unsettles him. He feels the weight of the burden upon him growing heavier with each passing moment.)

Kian: (his voice firming with resolve)
"I don't care about your games. I'm going to the Heart of the Moon, and nothing will stop me."

Shadow: (his eyes narrowing, his smile returning, colder now)
"Then so be it. But remember this, Kian. The shadow that walks beside you is not your enemy. It is your greatest ally… or your final downfall."

(The Shadow raises a hand, his fingers curling as if summoning the night itself. The air around Kian grows heavy, the temperature dropping as the shadows deepen. But before Kian can react, the man vanishes into the darkness with a soft, mocking laugh, leaving only the faintest echo of his words behind.)

Kian: (panting, his mind racing, confusion swirling in his chest)
"Who… what was that?"

(He stands alone in the clearing, the wind howling around him once more. But something has changed. The air feels thicker now, charged with a dangerous energy. Kian knows that his journey has only just begun, but the path ahead is even more uncertain and treacherous than before.)

(Kian looks up at the towering peaks of the mountains, the dark sky stretching endlessly above him. He has no choice now but to continue. But the Shadow's words linger in his mind, a warning that he can't shake. As he moves forward, the weight

*The Shadow's Edge*

of his destiny presses down on him with a new sense of urgency. The Heart of the Moon may hold the key to saving the clans, but it also holds the potential for unimaginable destruction.)

Kian: (to himself, his voice filled with quiet determination)
"I don't know who you are, or what you want from me… but I will find the Heart of the Moon. And I will make sure the Claw never falls into the wrong hands."

(With a deep breath, Kian continues down the winding path, his every step now laced with the promise of danger. The wind carries whispers, the shadows seem to stir with a life of their own, and the unknown waits at the edge of the mountain pass. The game has only just begun.)

**Four**

# Whispers of Betrayal

Scene: The dimly lit interior of an ancient inn perched on the edge of a forgotten town, a place where even the stars seem hesitant to shine. The wooden beams above creak under the weight of time, and the air is thick with the scent of damp earth and burning firewood. The flickering candlelight casts long shadows on the walls, creating an unsettling atmosphere. KIAN, weary from his journey, sits at a small table in the corner of the room. His eyes are sharp, scanning the inn's patrons—rough men cloaked in cloaks, eyes glinting with suspicion, faces drawn tight with secrets they refuse to share. He can feel it—something in the air tonight, a tension so thick it nearly suffocates him. His instincts, honed from years of survival in the wild, tell him that this is no ordinary night. The whispers of betrayal, faint at first, are now louder, creeping around him like the insidious shadow of a storm about to break.

Kian: (muttering to himself, his eyes never leaving the patrons)
"Something's wrong. I can feel it. The air's too still... too heavy."

(He grips the hilt of his dagger, the worn leather of the handle comforting beneath his fingers. His mind races as he recalls the Shadow's warning—the cryptic words about allies and enemies intertwining. The Heart of the Moon... he needs to reach it. But in this town, surrounded by unknown faces, he feels the weight of a thousand eyes upon him.)

Innkeeper: (approaching Kian's table with a forced smile, the lines around his eyes betraying years of worry)
"You look like a man with something on his mind, traveler. Care for a drink? Something to ease that frown of yours?"

Kian: (looking up at the innkeeper, studying his face carefully)
"Water. And keep it quiet. I don't need any trouble."

Innkeeper: (nodding with a hint of unease, his voice low)
"Of course. You'll find no trouble here... for now. But there are things in this town that you should know about. People come and go, but not all are who they seem."

(The innkeeper walks away without another word, leaving Kian with a feeling of dread gnawing at his stomach. He watches the innkeeper disappear into the shadows behind the bar, where he exchanges murmured words with a hooded figure. Kian's senses sharpen. The whispers of betrayal grow louder, like distant voices carried on the wind. His heart rate quickens. He doesn't know who to trust anymore, but he knows one thing—he must keep his guard up.)

(Moments later, the innkeeper returns with a tankard of water, setting it down on the table with a quiet clink. He lingers a moment longer, his eyes darting nervously toward the back of the inn before leaning in closer.)

Innkeeper: (whispering, his voice low and urgent)
"You're not the first to come searching for the Heart of the Moon, you know. There have been others... and they didn't leave with good intentions."

(Kian's pulse spikes, his eyes narrowing as he listens intently.)

Kian: (his voice calm, but his eyes sharp)
"What do you mean? Who else has come here?"

Innkeeper: (glancing over his shoulder, his voice barely above a whisper)
"Men with dark eyes and darker hearts. They came not long ago, asking questions—about the moon, about the Heart, about things that are better left forgotten. They didn't stay long, but they left their mark. And now, there's a... tension in the air. The town is uneasy. And those men—those wolves—they're still watching. They've got their eyes on you."

(Kian sits up straighter, the innkeeper's words sinking deep into his gut. His eyes flick to the shadows in the far corners of the room, where the patrons continue to whisper among themselves, eyes flicking over to him from time to time. He knows he is being watched.)

Kian: (in a low, measured voice)
"Who are they? Who sent them?"

(The innkeeper hesitates, his eyes darting nervously once more. He shakes his head, his voice barely audible.)

Innkeeper:
"I don't know who they work for... but I know this—there are rumors that they're looking for someone. A wolf, like you. They'll do anything to stop whoever stands in their way."

(A chill runs down Kian's spine as the innkeeper walks away. The words "anything to stop" echo in his mind, growing louder with each passing second. He's not alone in this search for the Heart of the Moon. And whoever these men are, they are not just after the Heart—they're after him.)

(Kian takes a deep breath, trying to steady his racing thoughts. He knows he can't stay in the inn for long. The tension in the air is suffocating, and he can feel eyes on him from all corners of the room. His instincts scream at him to leave. But as he stands, preparing to head for the door, a voice calls out from behind him.)

Voice: (sharp and commanding)
"Leaving so soon, traveler?"

(Kian spins around, his hand already reaching for his dagger. Standing in the doorway of the inn is a man, tall and imposing, his features shadowed by the low light. His eyes are dark—almost unnatural—and his lips curl into a smile that doesn't reach his eyes. There's something about him, something predatory, that makes Kian's stomach tighten.)

Kian: (coldly, narrowing his eyes)
"Who are you?"

Stranger: (stepping forward, his movements smooth and deliberate)
"Names aren't important, are they? What matters is that you're here. And that's what's interesting, isn't it? A lone wolf, wandering in the dark, looking for answers. Looking for the Heart. But be careful, Kian… answers aren't always what they seem."

(Kian's grip tightens on the dagger's hilt, his senses flaring as the man approaches. The words "answers aren't always what they seem" ring in his mind, and his pulse quickens. Something about this man feels wrong, like he's toying with Kian, leading him down a path from which there may be no return.)

Kian: (his voice low and filled with suspicion)
"I don't know who you are, but if you've come for trouble, you've found it."

Stranger: (laughing softly, his voice a low, almost melodic sound)
"Trouble? No, no, not trouble. I'm here to offer you a… choice. You can keep searching for the Heart, following that winding path that will lead you to nothing but ruin. Or you can come with me, and I'll show you something that might change everything. It's your decision."

## Whispers of Betrayal

(The man's eyes gleam with something unsettling, as though he already knows what Kian will choose. The room seems to close in on Kian, the air heavy with the weight of the stranger's words. Kian knows that this moment will define everything.)

Kian: (his voice steady, eyes cold)
"I don't trust you. And I don't trust your offer."

Stranger: (nodding slowly, as if he expected nothing less)
"Ah, but trust is a fragile thing, isn't it? Sometimes, betrayal comes from the places you least expect. Perhaps… you should reconsider."

(Before Kian can respond, the man turns sharply and strides toward the door, his figure swallowed by the darkness outside. Kian stands frozen for a moment, his mind racing, trying to make sense of everything. The offer, the warning, the dark truth behind the stranger's words. A betrayal is coming. He can feel it in his bones.)

(Kian glances around the inn once more, the unease settling into his chest like a stone. The patrons, the innkeeper, the stranger—all of them are connected to something far darker than he could have imagined. He cannot stay here. He must keep moving. The Heart of the Moon is still out there, but now, he must be wary of the shadows lurking in the corners of his world. And of the people who would sell him out for their own gain.)

Kian: (under his breath, to himself)
"Whispers of betrayal… they're everywhere. But I won't let

them stop me. Not now. Not ever."

(With a final glance at the door where the stranger disappeared, Kian walks out into the cold night, the weight of the world bearing down on him. But as the shadows close in around him, he knows one thing for sure: the path ahead will not be easy. And the stakes have just gotten much higher.)

**Five**

## *The Hunt Begins*

⁘

Scene: The moon, full and bright, hangs high in the night sky, casting a silvery glow over the vast expanse of the forest. The trees, ancient and towering, sway in the wind, their dark silhouettes forming a labyrinth of shadows. Beneath the canopy, the ground is damp, leaves crunching underfoot as KIAN moves stealthily through the underbrush. His senses are heightened, the scent of the forest overwhelming in his nostrils, yet underneath it, there is something else— something darker, more dangerous. The whispers from the inn, the warnings from the Shadow, and the cryptic stranger's words all swirl in his mind, making it impossible to focus on anything but the path ahead. He has been tracking these men—these wolves—who seek the Heart of the Moon, but now, something has changed. His prey is no longer just a shadow in the distance. They are close. Too close. And Kian can feel their eyes on him, even though he cannot see them.

Kian: (whispering to himself, his voice tense)
"I can feel them. They're here. They've been watching me."

(He pauses, crouching low in the underbrush, his eyes scanning the moonlit forest around him. The wind carries the scent of damp earth, pine, and… something else—something metallic, tinged with the scent of wolves. His heart rate quickens. The hunters are not just close—they are on his trail.)

Kian: (grimacing, his voice low and full of resolve)
"Not today. I won't let them catch me off guard."

(He rises slowly, moving like a shadow, blending into the night. Every step is calculated, measured, as he follows the faintest tracks left by the wolves—barely perceptible claw marks in the mud, the occasional broken branch, the disturbed foliage. His mind works quickly, piecing together the puzzle of their movements. They're smart, he can tell, but so is he. And he knows this forest better than anyone.)

(Suddenly, a snap of a twig. Kian freezes, his muscles coiled, ready to spring into action. He raises a hand to his nose, inhaling deeply, testing the air. The scent is stronger now—more distinct. He can smell the wolves. Not just one, but several. The pack. His heart races with adrenaline, but his mind remains sharp. There's no turning back now.)

Kian: (to himself, muttering under his breath)
"Focus. Stay sharp. You've got this."

(A soft rustling from behind him. He spins around, dagger

raised, but finds nothing. The forest is silent, eerily so. His skin prickles with the unmistakable feeling of being watched. He knows they're out there, hidden in the shadows, waiting for the perfect moment to strike.)

Kian: (calling into the darkness, his voice loud and firm)
"Come out, wolves. I know you're here."

(The silence hangs heavy in the air for a moment, and just as Kian begins to lower his guard, the sound of growling fills the air. It's low at first, the deep rumble of a threat. Then, from the shadows, three wolves emerge, their eyes glowing in the darkness. They are not ordinary wolves—these are creatures born of the hunt, their fur slick and black, their muscles rippling beneath their skin. Their teeth gleam in the moonlight, and their eyes burn with a fierce hunger. Kian doesn't hesitate. He shifts into his wolf form in an instant, the transformation seamless and fluid, his body becoming stronger, faster, more lethal.)

Kian: (growling low, his voice guttural, animalistic)
"You think you can catch me? You've made a mistake."

(The pack surrounds him, their eyes never leaving his. The leader, a massive black wolf with a scar running down his muzzle, steps forward, his snarl cutting through the air.)

Alpha Wolf: (his voice low, dripping with malice)
"You've been a thorn in our side for too long, boy. But it ends tonight."

Kian: (his lips curling into a snarl, his hackles raised)
   "We'll see about that."

(In a flash, the wolves lunge, their bodies a blur of speed and power. Kian reacts instinctively, dodging to the side just as the first wolf's teeth snap at his throat. He slashes with his claws, the sharp tips slicing through the air. One of the wolves yelps in pain, stumbling backward as blood stains the ground. But there's no time to celebrate. The alpha wolf is already circling, his eyes locked on Kian with deadly intent.)

Alpha Wolf: (laughing darkly, his voice filled with disdain)
   "You're fast, but you're not fast enough."

(The alpha lunges, his jaws open wide, aiming for Kian's throat. But Kian is faster. He ducks low, spinning on his hind legs and launching himself into the air. His claws dig into the alpha's side as he flips over him, landing with a soft thud behind the pack. The alpha howls in pain, spinning around, but Kian is already in motion again.)

Kian: (his voice low and filled with determination, even as he fights)
   "You're not my enemy. Not yet."

(But the wolves don't listen. They're relentless, their primal instincts driving them forward with vicious precision. Kian continues to fight, each movement a dance of survival. The ground beneath his paws is slick with blood now, his own wounds starting to sting, but he doesn't slow. He can feel their desperation, the need to bring him down. But Kian won't give them the satisfaction.)

(The battle rages on, Kian darting in and out of the shadows, striking when they least expect it. The wolves grow more aggressive, their attacks more calculated. It's clear they're not just hunting him—they're trying to wear him down. And as the seconds tick by, Kian realizes they're succeeding. His movements are starting to slow, his breath coming in ragged gasps. The alpha wolf circles him, his eyes gleaming with dark satisfaction.)

Alpha Wolf: (his voice cold and threatening)
  "You're running out of time, wolf. We're closing in. And when we catch you, there will be nowhere to run."

(Kian's mind races, but his body is growing heavier with each passing moment. The wolves are too many, too strong. He knows he can't take them all on at once. But there's one thing they don't know. Kian still has the element of surprise.)

(With a sudden burst of energy, Kian breaks into a full sprint, darting through the trees, weaving between the shadows. The pack gives chase, howling in fury as they pursue him. Kian's heart pounds in his chest, the sound of his own breath the only thing he can hear. But he knows he has to lead them away, to draw them into a trap. He pushes himself harder, faster, until he can see the faint outline of a cliff up ahead. The wind picks up, howling through the trees, carrying with it the scent of rain. The moment has come.)

(Without warning, Kian changes direction, veering sharply to the right and leading the pack straight toward a steep drop. The wolves howl in surprise, but it's too late. As they close in on him, Kian leaps from the edge of the cliff, his powerful form soaring through the air. The wolves follow, too focused on their prey to realize the danger until it's too late. The first wolf tumbles over the edge, howling in terror as he falls into the dark abyss below.)

Kian: (panting heavily as he lands gracefully on the opposite side of the cliff, looking back with cold eyes)
"Not today."

(The remaining wolves screech to a halt at the edge, their eyes wild with rage and disbelief. They pace back and forth, unable to follow. The alpha wolf lets out a roar of frustration, his eyes burning with fury. Kian doesn't give them a second glance. He knows the fight isn't over yet, but for now, he's gained the upper hand.)

(He turns and begins to move swiftly through the forest once more, his heart still pounding, his senses alert for any signs of danger. The hunt is far from over, and the pack won't give up easily. But Kian knows one thing now—they underestimate him. And that will be their downfall.)

Kian: (to himself, his voice filled with a cold resolve)
"This hunt has only just begun. And I'm not done yet."

(The night closes in around him, the forest dark and quiet once more. But Kian knows this: the stakes have never been higher, and the wolves will stop at nothing to catch him. But he won't stop either. The Heart of the Moon is still out there, and Kian will find it. No matter what it takes.)

**Six**

# Tides of the Moon

Scene: The ocean stretches out endlessly before Kian, its dark waters shimmering beneath the pale light of the full moon. Waves crash against the jagged rocks, their deafening roar filling the night air. The scent of saltwater mixes with the briny tang of the wind, but there's something else in the air—a heaviness, an anticipation. Kian stands at the cliff's edge, the ocean churning below him, as if the earth itself is holding its breath. The moon above casts its silvery glow upon the scene, its reflection dancing on the surface of the water. Kian's heart beats heavily in his chest, and he can feel the pull of something ancient, something powerful, emanating from the depths. The Heart of the Moon is close. He can feel it in his blood, in the very marrow of his bones. But so are his enemies. They are never far behind, and the stakes are higher than ever. The tides are shifting—and with them, the course of his destiny.

Kian: (his voice low, a whisper to the night wind)
  "The tides call. The Heart is near, but so are they."

(He steps closer to the edge, peering out at the inky darkness below. The wolves that hunted him in the forest are still somewhere out there, their scent lingering in the wind like a shadow. But Kian knows they won't find him tonight. Not here. Not with the moon high above, casting its light upon the land. There's something sacred about this place—a pull, an energy that Kian can't quite understand, but he knows it's connected to the Heart of the Moon. It's the only reason he's here, standing on this cliff with the ocean crashing below him. The tide, he can feel, is moving in a way it hasn't in centuries. A harbinger. The beginning of the end—or perhaps the beginning of something new.)

(The sound of a branch cracking behind him snaps Kian back to reality. He spins around, his hand instinctively reaching for the dagger at his side, eyes scanning the darkened forest at his back. But it's only the wind, playing tricks on him. His pulse slows, but his senses remain heightened. The wolves are still out there, and the forest is thick with shadows.)

(He takes a deep breath, closing his eyes for a moment, letting the waves crash over him with their rhythmic sound. His mind shifts, focusing on the task at hand: finding the Heart of the Moon. It's said to be hidden in a cavern beneath the sea, guarded by creatures older than time itself. A cave of stone, ancient and secret, where the tides meet the earth—and where the moon's power is strongest.)

Kian: (muttering to himself, his voice carrying across the wind)
"Under the sea… beneath the waves. The Heart is there, but how do I reach it?"

(The sound of approaching footsteps interrupts his thoughts. A figure steps from the shadows of the trees, a cloak billowing behind them in the wind. Kian's body tenses, his hand still on the dagger, his eyes narrowing as the figure steps closer.)

Kian: (coldly, his voice steady despite the tension building in his chest)
"Who's there?"

(The figure steps into the moonlight, revealing themselves to be a woman, tall and graceful, her long dark hair fluttering around her face as the wind picks up. She looks at Kian with a mix of curiosity and something else—a knowing, as though she has been waiting for him.)

Woman: (her voice smooth, almost melodic)
"You're far from your pack, wolf. What brings you to these shores?"

Kian: (his eyes flick to the woman's hands, looking for any signs of a weapon, his voice cautious)
"I'm not here to speak of my pack. I'm here for something… more important."

Woman: (nodding as if she already knew, her expression unreadable)
"You seek the Heart of the Moon, don't you?"

(Kian's heart skips a beat. There's no denying the truth now. This woman knows exactly what he's after. His fingers tighten around the dagger's hilt, but he keeps his expression neutral, his voice hard.)

Kian: (sternly)
"Who are you? And how do you know that?"

Woman: (stepping closer, her gaze unwavering, as if she's assessing Kian's every move)
"I know much more than that. But names don't matter. What matters is that you're in the right place at the right time. The Heart of the Moon is not just a treasure to be claimed. It is a force, a power beyond your understanding. And the ocean calls for it—just as it calls for you."

(Kian's brow furrows. The woman's words make something deep inside him stir—an ancient truth he's not quite ready to face. His instincts tell him she's not an enemy, but there's still something dangerous about her. Something that doesn't quite sit right.)

Kian: (his voice measured, but with a hint of impatience)
"Enough with the riddles. What do you want from me?"

Woman: (smiling slightly, a flash of something wild in her eyes)
"I don't want anything from you, Kian. I want you to understand what you're dealing with. The Heart of the Moon is not a gift—it's a choice. And that choice will shape the future of the clans. The tides of the moon are shifting, and with them, everything will change. The question is, will you be ready when

the wave breaks?"

(The woman's words hang in the air, and for a moment, Kian feels as though the entire world is holding its breath. He turns his gaze back to the ocean, feeling the weight of her words settle deep within him. The Heart of the Moon is no simple object—it is a force, a power with the potential to shift the very balance of the world. Kian knows the wolves who are hunting him want the Heart for themselves, to control it, to wield its power. But he's starting to suspect that there is much more at play here—something far greater than any one pack or any one wolf.)

Kian: (his voice low, almost a whisper)
"What happens if I don't find it? What happens if it falls into the wrong hands?"

Woman: (her eyes darken, her expression solemn as she looks out toward the sea)
"Then the tides will break. And everything you've known will drown beneath the waves. The Heart of the Moon is the balance between light and dark, between the earth and the sea. Without it… the wolves will tear themselves apart. The clans will fall. And the world will descend into chaos."

(Kian feels the weight of her words settle into his chest, like a stone sinking in water. He turns his gaze to the sea once more, the moonlight reflecting off the waves, casting everything in an ethereal glow. The woman's words resonate with a deep truth he can't ignore. The Heart of the Moon is more than just a powerful artifact—it's the key to the survival of the clans, the key to their very existence.)

Kian: (after a long pause, his voice hard with resolve)
"Then I have no choice. I will find it. No matter the cost."

Woman: (nodding slowly, her eyes softening just slightly, but there's a sadness in them that Kian can't quite place)
"You think you have a choice. But remember, Kian, the tides are not kind to those who are unprepared. And the moon… it doesn't always shine on those who seek it."

(The woman's words seem to echo in the air, like the cry of the wind itself. Kian's heart beats faster, his pulse quickening as the weight of the task ahead settles in his bones. He doesn't have time to waste. The Heart of the Moon is close. But so are the wolves. And if he doesn't move quickly, the world will fall into darkness.)

Kian: (turning away, his voice filled with determination)
"I will be ready."

(Without another word, he begins to move, his footsteps quick and sure. The woman watches him for a moment, her gaze unreadable. But as Kian takes one last glance back at her, he sees something flicker in her eyes—a warning, perhaps. A sign of things to come.)

(The wind picks up again, howling over the cliffs, as the ocean churns beneath him, its waves crashing with increasing ferocity. The tides of the moon are shifting, and the world is changing. The hunt has begun, but this is only the beginning. Kian

*Lunar Claw*

knows that whatever happens next, he will need every ounce of strength, courage, and wisdom he has to survive what is to come. The moon will guide him—but only if he can survive the storm that's about to break.)

**Seven**

# Through the Fire

Scene: The night is heavy with the scent of burning wood. The air is thick with smoke as Kian stands at the edge of the clearing, watching as the village he once called home burns in front of him. The crackling flames lick the sky, casting a fiery glow that reflects off the glassy surface of the river nearby. His heart pounds in his chest, not just from the inferno before him, but from the knowledge that the wolves, the very pack that had been hunting him, are the ones responsible. They came in the night, with fire in their eyes and violence in their hearts, and now there's nothing left but ashes. Kian's blood boils, a primal urge rising in his chest. The village is gone, and with it, a part of him. But his mind is focused, his purpose clear. He needs to find the Heart of the Moon—and the wolves will not stop until they have it. The hunt isn't just for the Heart anymore. It's personal.

Kian: (whispering under his breath, his voice tight with rage) "This... this can't be how it ends."

(He steps forward, the heat from the flames warming his skin, but it doesn't reach his heart. His eyes scan the horizon, looking for any sign of movement—any sign of the wolves who did this. The fire illuminates the forest around him, casting long shadows, and he knows the wolves are still out there. He can feel them, like a dark cloud hanging over him, waiting for the right moment to strike.)

(In the distance, he hears the howl of a wolf, its mournful cry echoing through the smoke-filled night. Kian's instincts sharpen. His mind races with questions—why burn the village? What do they gain from this destruction? What's the connection to the Heart of the Moon?)

(As Kian moves deeper into the forest, the smell of burning pine mingles with the sharp scent of blood. His heightened senses pick up the faintest trace of something more—something ancient, something powerful. The Heart of the Moon is near. But so is the danger. The pack won't stop until they have it, and now, they know Kian is a threat to their plans.)

Kian: (gritting his teeth, his voice low and determined) "They want war? Fine. I'll give them one."

(As he moves forward, Kian's mind flashes to the woman he met on the cliffs—the one who spoke of the tides of the moon and the terrible cost of finding the Heart. The words she left him with linger in his mind, like a warning that has now taken root in his heart.)

Kian: (to himself, as his eyes scan the treeline)
"I have no choice. I must keep moving forward."

(But just as he takes another step, the ground beneath him trembles. The earth shakes with a violent force, and the trees around him begin to sway. Kian stops, his senses flaring as his heart races. From the shadows, a massive figure emerges—a wolf, larger than any he's ever seen before. It's not just any wolf. This one is covered in scars, its eyes burning with an intensity that makes Kian's blood run cold. The alpha of the pack.)

Alpha Wolf: (his voice a growl, his gaze fixed on Kian with a mixture of hatred and amusement)
"You've survived this long, wolf. But you will not survive the fire."

(With a sudden, terrifying speed, the alpha lunges at Kian, his massive form crashing through the trees. Kian reacts instinctively, diving to the side, his body moving like lightning. He lands hard on the ground, but before he can regain his footing, the alpha is on him again, his teeth snapping dangerously close to Kian's throat.)

Kian: (grunting as he rolls to the side, narrowly escaping the wolf's jaws)
"Not today, you bastard!"

(Kian springs to his feet, his claws flashing in the moonlight. He strikes, his talons cutting through the air, but the alpha is faster, dodging with ease. The two wolves circle each other, each waiting for the other to make a move. Kian's heart pounds in his chest, his breath coming in sharp gasps. The alpha is strong—stronger than Kian had anticipated. But there's no turning back now. This fight will decide everything.)

Alpha Wolf: (taunting, his voice low and vicious)
"You've come all this way, Kian. And for what? To die alone in the fire?"

Kian: (his voice a low growl, filled with rage)
"You won't break me. I will find the Heart. And when I do, I'll destroy you all."

(The alpha snarls, his eyes flashing with fury. He lunges again, his jaws wide, aiming for Kian's throat. But Kian is ready this time. He shifts with the grace of a panther, sidestepping the attack, and before the alpha can react, Kian's claws rake across his side. The alpha howls in pain, but there's no hesitation. He turns, his eyes burning with vengeance, and charges once more.)

(The battle between them rages on, each wolf moving with deadly precision, each strike meant to kill. Kian can feel the heat from the flames behind him, the fire lighting up the forest like a hellish landscape, but it's a distraction. His focus is on the alpha—on ending this, once and for all.)

(Just as the alpha lunges again, Kian feints to the side, ducking low. With a roar, the alpha crashes into a nearby tree, his body slamming into the trunk with a sickening crack. Kian's chance is here. He moves in a blur, his claws aimed for the alpha's throat.)

Kian: (growling through clenched teeth)
"This ends now."

(But before he can land the final blow, a sharp howl echoes through the forest, interrupting the moment. Kian's head snaps toward the sound, his eyes widening as he realizes what it means. Reinforcements. More wolves. And they're closing in fast.)

Kian: (panting, his voice full of frustration and determination)
"No…"

(The alpha, seizing the opportunity, pushes Kian off with a powerful shove, sending him crashing into the ground. The pack's howls grow louder as they draw closer, their predatory scent growing stronger. Kian struggles to rise, but the weight of his injuries—his bleeding side, his bruised ribs—makes it difficult. The fight is far from over, but the odds are no longer in his favor.)

Alpha Wolf: (his voice dripping with malice, as he rises to his feet)
"You're not strong enough, Kian. You never were. The Heart belongs to us. And we will burn this world down until it's ours."

(The alpha's words are like a knife to Kian's heart, but the fire within him only grows stronger. He refuses to let this be the end. He can hear the wolves approaching, feel their presence growing. But the moon's light is still there, still shining down, and in that light, Kian finds his resolve.)

Kian: (shouting, his voice filled with defiance)
 "I will not be your pawn!"

(With a fierce roar, Kian shifts back into his wolf form, his body rippling with power, his claws flashing as he charges. The wolves close in, but Kian has no fear now. He fights with a fury that blinds him to everything else—the fire, the pain, the pack closing in. He knows only one thing: he must protect the Heart. And if that means fighting through the fire itself, then so be it.)

(The flames roar higher now, the fire from the village creeping closer to where Kian and the alpha battle. The heat is unbearable, but it only fuels Kian's rage. He slashes at the alpha, his claws raking through fur and flesh, but the alpha retaliates, his teeth sinking deep into Kian's shoulder.)

Kian: (roaring in pain but undeterred, his eyes burning with fury)
 "You will not win."

(With a final, desperate push, Kian breaks free from the alpha's grip, using the last of his strength to launch himself at the massive wolf. His claws find their mark this time, and with a sickening growl, the alpha staggers back, blood pouring from the wound.)

(But the wolves are still coming. Kian knows he can't fight them all—not like this. He has to make a choice. His body aches, his breath ragged, but the Heart of the Moon is still out there, and he's come too far to turn back now.)

Kian: (to himself, through gritted teeth)
"Through the fire… I will rise."

(With that, Kian turns and bolts into the burning forest, leaping over flames, running as if the very earth beneath him will collapse if he stops. The wolves may have the fire, but Kian has something stronger—his will to survive.)

**Eight**

# The Witch's Secret

Scene: The moon hangs high in the sky, casting its pale light over the twisted trees of the forest. Kian's paws are bloodied from his escape through the fire, his muscles sore and strained from the brutal battle with the alpha. He's lost the pack—for now—but he knows they will return. The forest is silent, the night air thick with tension as he moves deeper into the shadows. There is only one place left to turn. The Witch.

(Kian's breath is shallow, the weight of the hunt pressing down on him, but he pushes forward. The woman with the secrets, the one who spoke of the tides and the Heart of the Moon, has told him that the answers he seeks lie in the heart of this cursed forest. He doesn't fully trust her, but he has no choice. The witch is his only lead.)

## The Witch's Secret

(The wind howls through the trees, carrying with it a strange scent, something both sweet and foul at the same time. Kian's hackles rise as he slows his pace, scanning the surrounding woods for any sign of danger. It feels like the forest itself is watching him—waiting. He knows he's getting close. The air grows heavier as he approaches the clearing, the smell of herbs and incense growing stronger. The Witch's hut comes into view, nestled between two gnarled trees, its crooked silhouette framed by the pale light of the moon.)

(He hesitates for a moment before stepping forward. The door to the hut is ajar, creaking softly in the breeze. Kian's instincts scream at him to turn back, but his need for answers outweighs his fear. With a steady breath, he pushes the door open and steps inside.)

Witch: (her voice low, echoing through the dark room as she stands by the flickering fire, her back to Kian)
"You've come at last, Kian."

Kian: (his voice a low growl, his eyes narrowing as he steps further into the room, his every movement cautious)
"How did you know I was coming?"

Witch: (she turns slowly, her face hidden by the shadow of her hood, her voice as cold and calm as the night air)
"I've known you were coming long before you stepped foot in this forest. The moon has whispered of your arrival. And the fire… it burns in your blood."

(Kian's hackles raise at her words, but he doesn't move, his eyes never leaving her. He has no time for games. The pack is still out there, and the Heart is slipping further from his grasp with every passing moment.)

Kian: (gritting his teeth, his voice sharp with impatience)
"I don't have time for riddles. I'm here for answers. The Heart of the Moon. Where is it?"

(The Witch tilts her head slightly, her lips curling into an almost imperceptible smile, though there is something dark in her eyes.)

Witch: (her voice like silk, smooth and alluring, yet carrying an undeniable weight)
"Ah, the Heart of the Moon. You seek it as if it is a simple trinket. But you are wrong, Kian. The Heart is not something to be claimed. It is something to be understood. It is a power greater than any one creature can wield."

(She steps forward slowly, her movement graceful, as if she is gliding through the air. Kian feels the weight of her gaze on him, her presence filling the room with a strange energy. He tightens his grip on the dagger at his side, his instincts telling him to be ready for anything.)

Kian: (his voice low and filled with resolve)
"I don't care what it is. I need to find it. It's the only way to stop them—to stop the wolves from tearing everything apart."

Witch: (laughs softly, the sound almost musical but laced with an edge of danger)

"You think finding the Heart will stop them? No, Kian. The wolves are the least of your concerns now."

(Kian's eyes narrow, his patience slipping. He steps forward, his stance tense.)

Kian: (firmly)
"Then tell me, Witch. What will stop them? What will stop this madness?"

(The Witch's smile fades as she looks at him with an unreadable expression. She raises one hand, gesturing to the darkened corners of the room where strange objects are strewn about—crystal balls, vials of strange liquids, and ancient tomes that seem to hum with an energy Kian can't quite place.)

Witch: (quietly, almost sorrowfully)
"It's not just the wolves you need to fear. The Heart of the Moon is not the only force at play here. There are ancient powers, older than the moon itself, that are awakening. The balance that the Heart once maintained is crumbling, Kian. The tides are no longer stable. The wolves are only one part of the storm."

(Kian's blood runs cold as he listens to her words. The moon. The tides. The Heart. It's all connected, but he can't see the full picture yet. His mind races, trying to make sense of what she's saying.)

Kian: (his voice urgent, demanding answers)

"Then what do I do? How do I stop it? How do I stop all of this?"

(The Witch's eyes flicker with something Kian can't quite place—sadness, perhaps, or something darker. She moves toward a nearby shelf and pulls down an ancient book, its cover cracked and worn. She opens it to a page filled with cryptic symbols, tracing a finger along the edges.)

Witch: (her voice quiet, almost a whisper, as if the words carry a weight too heavy to bear aloud)
"The Heart of the Moon is not just an artifact, Kian. It is a key. A key to an ancient power that has been locked away for centuries. The wolves… they seek the Heart because they believe it will give them control. But they do not understand the truth. There are forces beyond their reach, forces that the Heart can either lock away or unleash. And if they succeed in claiming it, it will be the end of everything you know."

(Kian steps forward, his eyes locked on the pages of the book, but he can't make sense of the symbols. He's not a scholar. He's a hunter. A warrior. And yet, he knows that this is bigger than any battle he's ever fought.)

Kian: (his voice raw, desperate)
"Then why didn't you tell me this sooner? Why didn't you warn me about this?"

Witch: (her voice low, tinged with sorrow)
"Because you were not ready to hear it, Kian. You still aren't. The Heart is not just a weapon to wield. It is a choice. A choice

## The Witch's Secret

to either protect the world from the forces that would tear it apart—or to release them and watch as everything burns. You must choose, Kian. The wolves will not stop. But neither will the ancient powers that slumber beneath the earth."

(Kian's mind spins as he absorbs her words. The Heart is more than just a source of power. It's a key to something much darker—something that could destroy everything. He's not sure if he's ready for the responsibility, but he knows one thing for sure: he cannot let the wolves get their hands on it. He can't let anyone unleash what lies dormant in the Heart.)

Kian: (his voice shaking with resolve, though uncertainty lingers in his eyes)
"Tell me how to stop them. Tell me what I need to do."

(The Witch's eyes meet his, and for a moment, there's a flicker of something—recognition, perhaps. She nods slowly, closing the book and placing it back on the shelf.)

Witch: (softly, but with undeniable weight)
"To stop them, Kian, you must face the Heart itself. But beware—the Heart will not choose you unless you prove yourself worthy. And even if you do, you may not be able to control what comes with it."

(Kian's heart races as her words sink in. He knows what he must do—but what if he's not ready? What if he's walking into a trap?)

Kian: (his voice a whisper of doubt)

*Lunar Claw*

"How do I prove myself worthy?"

(The Witch turns her back to him, her face hidden in shadow once more as she begins to speak in a voice like the wind itself—soft and chilling.)

Witch: (quietly, as if reciting an old mantra)
"You must journey into the heart of darkness and face the truth within yourself. Only then will the Heart reveal its secrets. But remember, Kian, some truths are not meant to be known. Some powers are too great for any one soul to bear."

(Kian's breath catches in his throat. He doesn't fully understand her cryptic words, but he knows one thing: he has no choice. The Heart is out there, and if he doesn't find it first, the wolves will. And when they do, nothing will stop the destruction that follows.)

Kian: (his voice hard with determination)
"I will find it. I will control it."

(The Witch turns to face him, her eyes filled with an ancient, knowing sadness.)

Witch: (softly)
"Then go, Kian. But know this—the path you are about to walk will change you. And once you face the Heart, there is no turning back."

(Kian stands in the Witch's hut, the weight of her words heavy in the air. The moonlight outside seems to shimmer, as if the very world itself is watching him. He doesn't know what lies ahead, but he knows he can't stop now.)

Kian: (whispering to himself, his voice full of resolve)
"I'll walk through the fire if I have to. I'll do whatever it takes."

(And with that, Kian steps into the night, his heart heavy with the knowledge of what awaits. The Heart of the Moon is still out there. And time is running out.)

**Nine**

## *The Hidden City*

Scene: Kian's steps are heavy as he moves through the dense, mist-laden forest. His fur is matted with the remnants of the battle, his eyes bloodshot from exhaustion, but his resolve is unwavering. He's been tracking the whispers of the Heart of the Moon for days, following cryptic clues from the Witch, each one leading him deeper into a realm of shadows and ancient secrets. The air around him is thick, as though the very land holds its breath, waiting for something to happen. The moon, full and radiant, casts an eerie glow on the path ahead. His claws scrape the ground as he presses forward, the silence of the forest pressing in on him like a weight he cannot shake.

(The path narrows as Kian pushes through the trees, the underbrush growing denser, the shadows more oppressive. And then, just as his senses begin to dull with fatigue, something

## The Hidden City

shifts. The air seems to hum with an otherworldly energy, and the ground beneath his feet changes, becoming smoother, almost... deliberate. Kian pauses, his breath quickening. He's not alone.)

(The earth before him cracks with an ancient, creaking sound, and then a massive stone door begins to rise from the ground, revealing a hidden passageway. A faint, blue light emanates from within, casting shadows that seem to stretch and move with a mind of their own. Kian's heart skips a beat. He steps forward, cautiously, as the air grows colder, the scent of old magic hanging thickly in the atmosphere.)

Kian: (whispering to himself, his voice filled with awe)
   "This... this must be it."

(He steps into the passageway, the door closing silently behind him as if it were never there. The stone walls around him are covered in intricate carvings, symbols that seem to pulse with life. The air is thick with the scent of ancient dust, and the faint sound of water trickling somewhere deep within the earth echoes through the corridor. Kian's steps are soft, measured, as he moves deeper into the heart of this hidden place. The weight of history presses on him like a living thing.)

(As he reaches the end of the passage, the walls open up into a vast cavern, the size of a small city. The sight takes Kian's breath away. The cavern is bathed in an ethereal light, the source unknown, casting everything in a soft, otherworldly glow. Tall, stone buildings rise from the ground, their architecture unlike anything Kian has ever seen—shapes that seem to defy logic and bend the laws of nature. The city is silent, its streets empty, as if abandoned long ago. But Kian can feel it—the presence of something ancient, something watching.)

Kian: (his voice a low growl, barely above a whisper)
"Where is everyone?"

(His voice echoes, but there's no response. The city feels empty, yet full of unseen eyes. He walks cautiously through the streets, his senses on high alert. Every shadow, every flicker of movement, sets his pulse racing. The Heart of the Moon is somewhere here, hidden within the secrets of this city. He can feel it calling to him, an invisible thread pulling him deeper into the heart of the ruins.)

(As he moves through the city, the buildings seem to loom over him, their spires reaching toward the cavern's ceiling like claws. The streets are cracked, worn by time, and the remnants of long-abandoned banners hang limply in the air, their once vibrant colors faded to dust. There are no signs of life—no creatures, no people. It is as if the city has been forgotten by time itself.)

(Kian reaches a large central square, where a massive, stone fountain stands. The water is still, frozen in time. In the center of the fountain is a statue—an imposing figure, carved from the same stone as the buildings around him. It's a wolf, but not any wolf Kian has ever seen. The wolf is larger, its features more regal, its eyes empty but somehow knowing. It is the shape of a wolf, but something about it feels wrong, as though it is not meant to be here.)

## The Hidden City

(Kian steps closer, his instincts prickling with unease. The statue's eyes seem to follow him, and for a moment, the air grows colder, the silence deeper. His heart beats faster, the hairs on the back of his neck standing on end. He knows, instinctively, that this city holds secrets far beyond his understanding.)

Kian: (to himself, his voice tinged with both wonder and caution)
"What is this place?"

(As if in response, the ground trembles beneath his feet. Kian stumbles, his claws scraping against the stone as the city seems to come alive. The faint hum of ancient magic fills the air, vibrating through his body, rattling his bones. The fountain begins to glow, a soft blue light emanating from within its waters. The statue of the wolf shifts, its eyes glowing briefly before it becomes still once more.)

(The ground trembles again, and suddenly, Kian hears a voice—not in his mind, but in the very air around him, as if the city itself is speaking.)

Voice: (low, reverberating, ancient)
"Who dares to awaken the city of shadows?"

(Kian's breath catches in his throat. The voice is both everywhere and nowhere at once, and it chills him to his very core.)

Kian: (his voice shaky but determined)
"I am Kian. I seek the Heart of the Moon."

(The city seems to hold its breath as the voice responds, the tone now laced with something darker, something ancient.)

Voice: (echoing)
"The Heart of the Moon is not for the likes of you. It was never meant to be found. You tread on the sacred ground of those who have long since passed. What is it you seek, child of the wolf?"

Kian: (his voice steadying, though his heart pounds in his chest)
"I seek to stop the wolves. They are hunting for the Heart. If they find it, the world will burn."

(There's a long pause, the silence deafening. The city seems to shift around him, the air thick with tension. The voice speaks again, this time with an edge of warning.)

Voice: (almost a whisper)
"Your kind always seeks to control what should remain untouched. The Heart is a force of nature, Kian. It is not yours to command. It is a power far older than you can comprehend."

(Kian's pulse quickens. He can feel it now—the pull of the Heart, stronger than ever. He knows that what he is about to face will change everything. The wolves, the pack—they are not the only threat. The Heart itself, and whatever ancient powers lie in this city, may be the true danger.)

(He takes a deep breath, steeling himself for what's to come. If the city has secrets, he's determined to uncover them. If the Heart is here, he will find it, no matter the cost.)

## The Hidden City

Kian: (his voice firm, despite the fear gnawing at his insides)
"I don't care what it takes. I will find the Heart. I will stop the wolves."

(The voice responds again, this time with a tone of finality.)

Voice: (darkly)
"Then you will learn the true price of the Heart, Kian. The city's curse is upon you now."

(Before Kian can react, the ground shifts violently beneath him. The city seems to wake from its slumber, its once still streets now trembling with energy. The fountains begin to bubble, the air crackling with power. Kian takes a step back, his senses heightened, his claws poised for whatever comes next.)

(In the distance, figures begin to emerge from the shadows. At first, they are only shapes—shifting forms that move like smoke. But as they draw closer, Kian can see them clearly: they are wolves, but not like any wolves he has seen before. Their eyes glow with the same blue light as the fountain, and their fur shimmers with an ethereal glow. They are ancient, their forms twisted by time and magic, their movements unnatural. They are guardians of this place—protectors of the Heart.)

(Kian's heart races as the wolves approach, their eyes fixed on him. He knows now that his journey is far from over. The true test is just beginning.)

Kian: (his voice a low growl, his stance ready)
"If you think you can stop me, then try."

(The wolves snarl, their voices like thunder, but before they can charge, the city itself seems to respond, the stone walls shifting and closing around them, trapping them in a web of ancient magic. Kian takes a deep breath, his claws itching for the fight, but he knows one thing for certain: the Heart of the Moon is here, and whatever it takes, he will claim it.)

(The Hidden City is alive, and it is not going to make it easy for him.)

**Ten**

# Echoes of War

Scene: The city hums with an eerie quiet. The wolves stand in a loose formation around Kian, their glowing eyes fixed on him, their presence a constant reminder of the ancient forces at play in this forsaken place. The air is thick with tension as the ground beneath them rumbles ever so slightly, the stone walls shifting in response to the wolves' power. The Guardians of the Heart. These creatures are not like the pack Kian has hunted for so long; they are beings of the old magic, twisted and forged by time itself. And they stand between him and the Heart.

(Kian's heart pounds in his chest, his breath steady but sharp. The wolves around him are silent, their forms flickering in the ethereal light. The weight of their gaze is oppressive, and every instinct inside him is telling him to fight, to run. But he knows that this is the moment that will define everything. There is no turning back now.)

Kian: (his voice is steady but tense, filled with the quiet defiance of one who has come too far to retreat)
"You don't scare me."

(The nearest wolf, a massive creature with eyes like molten silver, steps forward. Its fur ripples with an unnatural energy, shimmering like the light of the moon itself. It bares its fangs in a silent growl, but it does not move to attack. Instead, it watches him, its eyes probing, as if searching for something—perhaps a weakness, perhaps something deeper.)

Wolf: (its voice is deep, like the rumbling of thunder in the distance, its words hanging heavy in the air)
"You think you understand, Kian. You think you've come to claim the Heart of the Moon. But you are nothing more than a child playing with fire."

(The other wolves shift, their eyes flickering with agreement. They move slowly, cautiously, like predators circling their prey. Kian's body tenses, his claws aching for release, but he knows that fighting these creatures will not be as simple as an instinctual hunt. There is more at stake here than just a battle for survival.)

Kian: (his voice low, his eyes narrowing as he glares at the wolf in front of him)
"I've walked through fire, and I'll walk through hell if I have to. I'm here for the Heart. And I'll do whatever it takes to stop you."

(The wolf's lips curl into a twisted smile, revealing sharp teeth that glint in the soft, otherworldly light. The air around them crackles with an unsettling energy, and the city itself seems to respond to the tension, the stone walls vibrating with the resonance of ancient power.)

Wolf: (almost pityingly)
"You think the Heart is your salvation? It is nothing but a tool. A weapon meant to bring the end. The wolves may seek it for power, but they do not understand its true purpose. You are a fool to think you can control it."

(Kian's eyes flicker with anger, his chest tightening as he steps forward, refusing to back down.)

Kian: (his voice sharp, his every word heavy with resolve)
"I don't care about power. I care about stopping the wolves. I care about stopping this war."

(At the mention of war, the wolf's eyes flash, and it growls low in its throat, its posture shifting. The other wolves seem to tense at the word, as if the very mention of the war stirs something deep within them.)

Wolf: (its voice growls with a warning edge)
"You think you know what a war is? You think you understand the bloodshed and the destruction that follows? You are blind, Kian. This war… it has been fought for centuries. It is the war of the old gods, the war of the forces that created us, the war of the Heart itself."

(Kian falters for a brief moment, uncertainty flickering in his mind, but he pushes it away. The wolves want him to be afraid. They want him to doubt himself. But he cannot. He has come too far.)

Kian: (his voice firm, unwavering in its determination)
"Then tell me, if you think you know so much, what is the war really about? What is the Heart, and why is it so important?"

(The wolf's eyes narrow, and it tilts its head, as if considering the question. The silence stretches, heavy and pregnant with the promise of something terrible. Then, with a soft snarl, the wolf speaks again, its words carrying the weight of ancient knowledge.)

Wolf: (its voice laced with a mixture of sorrow and rage)
"The Heart is not a thing to be understood. It is a force—a will of its own, older than the wolves themselves. It was forged at the beginning of the world, when the first gods walked the earth. And it has been hidden away for centuries because its power is beyond comprehension. The Heart… it binds the very fabric of reality. It controls the tides of magic, the flow of time, the fate of the world itself. And now… it calls to you, Kian. It has chosen you."

(Kian's stomach lurches at the wolf's words. The Heart isn't just an object—it's a force, a will that could control everything. And if it has chosen him, then what does that mean? What has he become in its eyes?)

Kian: (his voice strained, his thoughts racing as he speaks)

*Echoes of War*

"What do you mean, it has chosen me? I don't—"

(Before Kian can finish, the city trembles again, this time more violently. The ground cracks, splitting apart as the walls groan and shift. The wolves growl, their hackles raised, and the air grows thick with the scent of magic. The fountain in the central square begins to glow more brightly, its waters swirling with a blue energy that seems to pulse with life. Kian's heart races, his instincts screaming at him to act.)

Kian: (yelling over the noise, his voice filled with urgency)
 "What's happening? What's going on?"

(The wolf's eyes gleam with a terrifying recognition, and it steps back, as if preparing for something inevitable.)

Wolf: (its voice filled with dark resignation)
 "The war has begun, Kian. The Heart calls for its chosen. The balance is shattered, and the tides of magic are rising. The old gods are awakening. And the wolves will lead the charge to claim what is theirs."

(Kian's blood runs cold at the wolf's words. The war the creature speaks of is not some ancient battle of the past—it is a war that is happening right now, a war that will tear the world apart. The wolves, with the Heart in their grasp, will unleash chaos unlike anything he has ever known.)

(The city shakes again, and Kian feels the energy surge around him, the magic coursing through the very stones beneath his feet. It is as if the city itself is alive, reacting to the coming storm. The sky above him begins to darken, and the full moon, once bright and shining, now appears shadowed, as though something is blocking its light. A terrible sense of impending doom fills the air.)

Kian: (his voice sharp with fear and determination)
"I won't let you win. I won't let you destroy everything."

(The wolves laugh, a low, guttural sound that reverberates through the city like the rumble of thunder.)

Wolf: (mockingly)
"You think you can stop us, Kian? You think you can stop the tide of fate? The Heart is already awakening, and the war has already begun. You cannot stand against what is coming."

(Before Kian can respond, the earth beneath him splits open, and from the crack, a massive, dark figure rises—a creature that is neither wolf nor man, but something far older, a being of pure magic. Its eyes are black as night, and its body is made of shifting shadows and molten light. It is a god, an ancient force brought to life by the Heart itself.)

Kian: (his voice trembling, his body rigid with fear, but his mind racing with determination)
"What is that? What have you unleashed?"

Wolf: (its voice filled with awe and dread)
"That… that is the Echo of War. The manifestation of the Heart's power. It has come to awaken the old gods. And when it is fully awakened, the world will burn. The wolves will rise,

and nothing will stand in their way."

(Kian's mind is reeling. The Heart is not just a tool—it is a weapon, a force that can reshape the very world. And he is caught in its pull, destined to either control it or be destroyed by it.)

(With a deep breath, Kian steps forward, his claws digging into the stone as he prepares to fight—not just for survival, but for the future of everything he has ever known.)

Kian: (his voice cold, filled with the promise of destruction)
 "I won't let the Echo of War drown this world. I will stop you, no matter what it takes."

(The Echo of War roars, a sound that shakes the very foundations of the city, and the battle begins. The fate of the Heart, of the wolves, and of the entire world hangs in the balance as Kian faces the true enemy, one far beyond anything he could have imagined.)

**Eleven**

# Bloodlines Converge

Scene: The city trembles with the power of the Echo of War, the stone beneath Kian's paws vibrating in resonance with the ancient forces awakening all around him. The air is thick with the scent of magic, as the ground cracks open further, revealing jagged edges and glowing veins of energy. The Echo of War stands before him, towering and incomprehensible, its shadow stretching across the ruined city like a cloak of impending doom. Kian's heart pounds in his chest, each beat a reminder of the battle that is about to unfold. The wolves stand back, watching with an unsettling calm, their eyes gleaming with something almost… expectant. The time for words is over. The time for blood is at hand.

(Kian's breath comes in sharp, shallow gasps, his claws digging into the stone as he surveys the Echo of War. The massive creature before him is a manifestation of pure, unbridled power.

## Bloodlines Converge

Its eyes burn with an unnatural fire, its body a swirling mass of shadows and molten light. It is the embodiment of destruction, a force that seeks to bring the world to its knees. The wolves are its vanguard, and the Heart of the Moon is the weapon that will ignite the chaos.)

Kian: (his voice is steady but filled with a quiet fury as he squares his shoulders, preparing for the inevitable battle)
"I won't let you destroy everything. You think you can reshape the world with the Heart, but you're wrong. This ends here."

(The Echo of War lets out a low, guttural laugh that vibrates through the very air. Its voice is both thunderous and mocking, reverberating in Kian's bones.)

Echo of War: (its voice deep and unsettling, like the growl of an ancient beast)
"You speak of ending, Kian, but there is no ending. The war is inevitable. The Heart has chosen its champion, and the time for the wolves' reign is upon us. Your bloodline, your very essence, is tied to this fate. You cannot escape it."

(Kian's heart skips a beat. The mention of his bloodline makes his thoughts race. How could the Echo of War know about his lineage? What connection does he have to the ancient powers that control the Heart?)

Kian: (his voice sharp with confusion and anger, though he struggles to maintain his focus)
"What are you talking about? I'm not some puppet of fate!

I'll never follow you!"

(The Echo of War steps forward, its massive form shaking the ground beneath Kian's feet. The wolves around them remain still, their eyes watching with an intensity that borders on reverence. The creature's molten eyes fixate on Kian, and a smile curves its shadowy lips.)

Echo of War: (its voice colder now, dripping with menace)
"You don't realize it, do you? You are more than just a wolf, Kian. You are the key. The Heart has been waiting for a bloodline to awaken its true potential. And your blood—your cursed, noble blood—is the final piece of the puzzle."

(Kian recoils, his mind racing. The words hit him like a blow to the chest. His bloodline? The Heart has been waiting for him? The very thought sends a shiver down his spine. But he can't let fear control him now. He has to understand what this creature means—and more importantly, how to stop it.)

Kian: (his voice low, shaking with the weight of the revelation)
"What do you mean? What bloodline? My father... my mother... they never spoke of this."

(The Echo of War's eyes gleam with satisfaction, its smile widening as it savors Kian's confusion.)

Echo of War:
"The blood of the original shifters flows through you, Kian. The same blood that birthed the first wolves, the first shapeshifters. Your ancestors were more than just beasts—they

were the guardians of the Heart. But in their arrogance, they sealed it away. They sought to control its power, and in doing so, they doomed their bloodline to endless strife. Now, the Heart calls you to finish what they started. To claim it—or perish in the attempt."

(Kian's mind spins. His ancestors, the original shifters, the ones who had hidden the Heart away—they were not just any wolves. They had been powerful beings, capable of shaping reality itself. And now, Kian is tied to their legacy, forced to carry the burden of their mistakes.)

Kian: (his voice trembling with anger and disbelief, struggling to comprehend the magnitude of what he's hearing)
"No. This isn't my fight! I never asked for any of this. I don't want your war!"

(The Echo of War's laugh rumbles through the air like distant thunder, its body shifting in the light, growing even larger and more imposing. The shadows around it writhe and twist, as if alive.)

Echo of War: (its voice seething with disdain and cruel amusement)
"You think you have a choice? The war has already begun, Kian. Your blood has already been chosen. The wolves have waited for centuries, and now it is time for the bloodlines to converge. The Heart will awaken, and when it does, the world will kneel before it."

(Kian's chest tightens as the reality of what the creature is saying sinks in. He is tied to the Heart, tied to this ancient war that spans centuries. But he cannot, will not, accept that he is powerless in this. The wolves may think they have the power, but Kian has something they don't: the will to fight, to defy fate.)

Kian: (his voice firm, determination burning in his eyes)
"If you think you've already won, then you're wrong. I will fight you—we will fight you. The pack may not know it yet, but they will stand with me. I will not let this war destroy everything."

(The Echo of War's eyes narrow, its smile faltering for the briefest of moments. It's as if the creature is considering Kian's words, assessing the threat of defiance in his voice. But then the laughter starts again, louder, more mocking.)

Echo of War:
"You speak of unity, of defiance—but you cannot fight what is inevitable. You cannot rally those who have already chosen their side. The pack is already divided. They will turn on you the moment the Heart calls to them."

(Kian's heart clenches at the thought. The pack turning on him—that's exactly what he's been afraid of. The wolves have always been bound by their instincts, by their bloodlust. But Kian believes in the bond they share, believes that they can fight this together. He will not let the Echo of War's lies divide them.)

Kian: (his voice hardening, his claws digging deeper into the stone)

"I'll make them see the truth. You're the one who's lying. I won't let this power corrupt us. Not again."

(The Echo of War tilts its head, its gaze shifting from Kian to the surrounding wolves. They remain eerily still, their eyes glowing like embers in the night. The creature's voice drops to a whisper, its tone heavy with finality.)

Echo of War:
"Then you are truly a fool, Kian. For when the wolves' bloodline converges, it will not be for the sake of unity. It will be for war. Your bloodline will not save you. It will be your downfall."

(Before Kian can respond, the wolves around them begin to stir. A low growl ripples through the group, and Kian turns sharply, his body tense, ready for an attack. The pack's leader, a massive wolf with fur like midnight, steps forward, its eyes glowing with the same blue light as the Heart. It is clear—this wolf is not here to protect Kian. It is here to bring him to his knees.)

Leader of the Wolves: (its voice low and commanding, filled with authority)
"The Heart calls to us, Kian. You can no longer deny your destiny. The bloodlines converge, and the wolves will rise. Your defiance is meaningless."

(Kian's pulse quickens. His mind races, but his body is already reacting. The pack is splitting apart. The wolves are choosing their side, and Kian knows he must act now, before it's too late. He cannot allow the Echo of War to win. Not now, not ever.)

Kian: (his voice steady, his gaze fixed on the pack leader, his body poised for battle)
"You're wrong. This isn't over. Not by a long shot."

(The moment of hesitation between Kian and the pack leader stretches like a drawn bowstring, ready to snap. The air is thick with the promise of violence, of bloodshed, as the wolves begin to circle him, their eyes filled with a mix of loyalty to their kind and the call of the Heart. The fate of the pack, and of Kian himself, rests on the razor's edge.)

(The final, inevitable clash is about to begin. Kian's bloodline, his destiny, his survival—everything converges in this moment.)

## Twelve

## *The Wolf Within*

───·ᗢ·───

Scene: The air is thick with anticipation, a heavy stillness descending over the battlefield. The wolves stand at attention, their eyes glowing like molten embers, their forms poised for attack. Kian's heart hammers in his chest, the pulse of battle coursing through his veins. Before him stands the pack leader, the one who was once his ally, now his enemy. The bond they shared has shattered, and the Heart, pulsing with power, calls out to them both. The tension is unbearable, a thin thread waiting to snap, and in the distance, the shadow of the Echo of War looms, waiting for the final act of this ancient, doomed play to unfold.

(Kian stands alone at the edge of the ruins, the moon above casting its cold, silver light upon the scene. The wolves surround him, their eyes fixed, their bodies tense. The pack leader, a towering figure with fur as black as the void, steps forward, its fangs bared in a silent challenge. Kian's body tenses, his instincts screaming to fight, but he forces himself to stay calm. He knows this is no ordinary battle. This is not just a fight for survival—it is a battle for control of the Heart, for the very soul of the pack.)

Kian: (his voice steady, but laced with the weight of what's about to come)
"You don't have to do this. The Heart is not what you think it is. It will only bring destruction, not power."

(The pack leader's glowing eyes narrow, its posture shifting from one of aggression to one of sorrowful inevitability. The creature tilts its head slightly, as if listening to Kian's words, but then the low growl begins to rumble deep within its chest.)

Pack Leader: (its voice deep, a low growl that sends shivers down Kian's spine)
"You don't understand, Kian. You never did. The Heart is the only way to bring unity, to bring an end to the endless war. You've always been too weak to see it."

(The wolves around them shift slightly, their eyes flickering between Kian and their leader, as if torn between loyalty and the irresistible pull of the Heart's call. Kian's blood boils at the words, his anger rising like a firestorm inside him.)

Kian: (his voice raw, laced with both defiance and pain)
"You've been brainwashed by the same lies the Echo of War feeds to you. The Heart doesn't unify—it divides. It's a weapon of destruction, not salvation. You've been blinded by power!"

## The Wolf Within

(The pack leader's snarl deepens, the glow in its eyes intensifying. Its body ripples with dark energy, and for a moment, Kian can feel the very air around him shift, as if the pack itself is awakening to a darker, more primal hunger.)

Pack Leader: (its voice cold, carrying the weight of finality)
"You are a fool, Kian. You always were. The Heart chose you, but not to save us. It chose you because you are the key to unlocking its true potential. You are nothing more than a pawn in a game you don't understand. And now, you will die for your defiance."

(In the instant that the pack leader speaks, the wolves surge forward in unison, their forms blurring into motion as they move toward Kian. He doesn't have time to think—he can only react. His instincts kick in. His claws elongate, and a surge of primal energy erupts from deep within him. His body shifts, his senses heightening. His mind floods with clarity as the wolf within him awakens, roaring to life, more powerful than ever before.)

(With a swift motion, Kian lunges, his body moving faster than he's ever moved before. The first wolf in the pack leaps toward him, its fangs bared, but Kian sidesteps with fluid grace, slashing with his claws and striking the creature's side. It yelps in pain but quickly recovers, turning to face him with renewed ferocity.)

Kian: (his voice a guttural growl, his body trembling with the raw power surging through him)
"You're making a mistake."

(He stands firm, the pack closing in around him. The wolves are faster, stronger, their primal instincts honed by centuries of battle. But Kian is no longer the young wolf they once knew. He is something more, something that burns with the fury of a thousand suns. The wolf within him is no longer just a part of him—it is him. And it will not be denied.)

(The pack leader snarls, its voice rising above the chaos, calling to the wolves to attack in unison. They move together, a tide of fur and fangs, intent on tearing Kian apart. But he is ready. He channels every ounce of his strength, every shred of his will, as the Heart's power begins to course through his veins.)

Pack Leader: (its voice shaking with frustration and anger)
"You are nothing without us, Kian. You can't defeat us. We are the pack. We are the Heart!"

(Kian's eyes narrow, his gaze locked onto the pack leader's. In that moment, he sees it—sees the truth behind the mask of power. The pack leader is not acting out of strength, but out of desperation. It has been consumed by the Heart's call, just as the wolves around it have been. The pack is divided, but the leader cannot see it. It is too lost in its own power to realize that the unity it seeks will only come through destruction.)

(The wolves close in, their fangs glinting in the dim light, their growls deafening. But Kian stands tall, his claws gleaming with the ethereal power of the Heart. The wolf within him—the true wolf—is no longer an instinct to be controlled. It is a force of nature, untamable and unstoppable. With a roar that echoes through the city, Kian leaps into the fray.)

## The Wolf Within

(He moves faster than the eye can see, his body a blur of motion as he fights with the fury of the storm. Every strike, every blow, lands with devastating force, but the wolves do not relent. They press forward, determined to overwhelm him. Kian can feel the energy of the Heart surging within him, fueling his every movement, but there is something darker at play here—something that calls to him from deep within the shadows of his own soul.)

(As the battle rages on, Kian begins to lose himself in the frenzy of the fight. His thoughts blur, and his mind drifts, until he is no longer fighting for survival. He is fighting for the Heart. The Heart is his, and he will stop at nothing to control it.)

(But just as the chaos reaches its peak, Kian hears a voice—a voice in his mind, soft but insistent. It is a voice he recognizes, one that calls to him from the depths of his soul.)

Voice: (whispering in his mind, a voice that carries both warmth and cold)
 "Kian… remember who you are. You are not just a weapon. You are not just a tool for the Heart's power. You are a wolf. And you must choose who you fight for."

(The voice pierces through the bloodlust, cutting through the fog of battle like a beacon in the night. Kian's heart skips a beat, and for the first time in what feels like forever, he pauses. He halts in mid-motion, his claws just inches from the throat of the pack leader.)

Kian: (his voice trembling, torn between the wolf inside him and the reality of what he's becoming)

"I… I don't know anymore."

(The wolves slow, their movements faltering as they sense Kian's hesitation. The pack leader growls, its eyes burning with fury, its teeth flashing as it snarls in frustration.)

Pack Leader: (its voice rising with rage, its power surging with the force of an avalanche)

"You are weak, Kian! This is your destiny! You cannot resist it! You are nothing without the Heart!"

(But Kian's mind is no longer clouded by rage. He can feel the truth now, deep within him. He is not just a wolf. He is a warrior—a protector of the pack, a guardian of the world. The Heart cannot control him, no matter how powerful it is. He is the wolf within, and nothing can extinguish the fire that burns in his soul.)

(With a roar of defiance, Kian breaks free from the grip of the Heart's call. His claws extend, his body shifts with the primal power of the wolf, and he charges forward, a blur of motion, intent on ending this madness once and for all.)

(The pack leader lunges to meet him, its fangs bared in a final, desperate attempt to destroy him. But Kian is faster, his every movement a strike of pure will. With a single blow, he disarms the leader, knocking it to the ground. The other wolves hesitate, confusion filling their eyes. The pack is fractured, and Kian knows that this battle is far from over. But for the first time, he feels the weight of his true power—the wolf within is no

## The Wolf Within

longer just a part of him. It is his strength, his salvation.)

(Kian stands over the fallen pack leader, his chest heaving, his claws glowing with the energy of the Heart. But the war is not yet won. The wolves still remain. The Heart still calls. And the battle is far from finished.)

**Thirteen**

# *The Thieves' Gambit*

Scene: The dim-lit streets of the hidden city are alive with whispers. Kian's senses are heightened, each footstep echoing through the narrow alleyways as he weaves through the shadows. His heart beats heavily, the anticipation of what is to come tightening around him like a vice. The pack's betrayal still stings, but he knows that time is running out. The Heart's power is growing stronger by the day, and with every passing hour, the wolves grow bolder, more dangerous. There is no choice left. Kian must find the Lunar Claw before it's too late. But there are others who seek it, too—others who are willing to do whatever it takes to claim its power.

(Kian reaches the heart of the city, where the streets are lined with rotting wood and broken stone. The buildings loom overhead like silent sentinels, their dark windows hiding the secrets of a long-forgotten past. He moves with purpose, his eyes scanning the shadows for any sign of danger. He is not alone in the city, not by a long shot. The thieves, mercenaries, and rogues that haunt these streets know all too well the value of a relic like the Lunar Claw. Kian can feel their eyes on him, watching, waiting. They have their own agendas—and they would kill to get their hands on the artifact.

(In the distance, a figure moves quickly through the gloom, their silhouette barely visible beneath a cloak. Kian's instincts flare, and his body tenses. It is not just a thief he's sensing—it's something far worse. He steps forward, silently as the wolf within him urges him onward. He must find this rogue before they find him.)

Kian: (whispering to himself as he crouches in the shadows) "Stay sharp, Kian. They're close."

(The figure draws nearer, moving with fluid grace, their steps silent as the night itself. The sound of fabric brushing against stone barely registers in the air as they pause, standing just outside an old, decrepit warehouse. The figure looks around, scanning the area before stepping forward and disappearing inside. Kian's breath catches in his throat, and without a second thought, he follows, slipping silently into the dark doorway behind them.)

(The inside of the warehouse is colder than the night air, and the scent of mildew and old wood fills Kian's nostrils. The walls are lined with crates, some of them stacked high, others abandoned and broken. A narrow shaft of moonlight pierces through the dust-covered window, casting a pale glow across

*Lunar Claw*

the room. The figure is there, rummaging through a pile of crates in the far corner.)

Kian: (his voice barely a whisper, filled with cold calculation)
"You're looking for something, aren't you?"

(The figure freezes, their head snapping toward Kian. Their eyes glow with a dim, eerie light, and a grin spreads across their face—too wide, too knowing.)

Rogue: (the voice soft but full of danger, tinged with amusement)
"Didn't expect company. I assume you're here for the same reason I am?"

(Kian's eyes narrow as he steps forward, the moonlight reflecting off his claws, the wolf within him sharpening his focus. This rogue is dangerous, but they are not his true target. Kian's instincts scream at him—this is more than just a thief. This person is working for someone, someone powerful. Someone who is also hunting for the Lunar Claw.)

Kian: (his voice laced with suspicion, but his stance unwavering)
"I don't know what you're after, but I'm not here for a chat. Get out of my way."

(The rogue laughs, the sound echoing eerily in the warehouse, bouncing off the stone walls.)

Rogue: (amused, mocking)

"How rude. But, you know, I have to admit, you're not entirely wrong. We're both after the same thing. The Lunar Claw. But I doubt you're the only one who's been searching for it. The game is bigger than you think, Kian."

(Kian's breath catches at the mention of the Lunar Claw. His eyes narrow, every muscle in his body tightening with the weight of the rogue's words. There's a familiarity to their tone—an insider's knowledge of something far more intricate than he'd first assumed. This rogue knows something he doesn't.)

Kian: (with a dangerous edge in his voice, his eyes burning with determination)
"Who are you working for? Who else is hunting the Claw?"

(The rogue's eyes gleam with something dark, something cold. They step closer, their every movement precise, calculated. Kian's muscles tense, every instinct telling him that this is the moment everything could unravel. The rogue might be the key to everything he's been searching for, but they could also be a deadly trap.)

Rogue: (their voice low, conspiratorial)
"You think you're the only one who knows of the Heart's power? You think you're the only one who has the bloodline to claim it? I've been watching you, Kian. I know what you're capable of—and so do they."

(Kian's pulse quickens. They are watching him—they? Who? Who could possibly know what he's been through, what he's seeking?)

Kian: (his voice low, threatening)

"I don't care who you think you know. I'm taking the Claw, and I'm stopping this madness. If you're in my way, I'll make you regret it."

(The rogue smirks, as if entertained by Kian's bravado. They take a step back, raising a hand to the shadows, and in an instant, several more figures emerge from the dark corners of the warehouse. Kian's eyes widen as he spots them—more thieves, mercenaries, and trained killers. Each one wears a dark cloak, and each one is armed, poised for a fight. Kian's body stiffens as he prepares himself for what's to come. They knew he would follow. This was a trap.)

Rogue: (grinning, their eyes glowing with malicious glee)

"Did you really think you could come here alone? The thieves' gambit isn't just about stealing from the rich—it's about survival. It's about alliances. And right now, we're the ones with the advantage."

(The other figures step forward, their weapons drawn. Kian's heart races, but his eyes remain steady. There's no room for doubt, no time for hesitation. If he's to survive this, he has to act fast.)

Kian: (his voice cold, a steely determination lacing every word)

"I don't need your help. But I'll gladly leave you all in pieces if you think you can stop me."

(The tension in the air is palpable as the thieves close in, circling around Kian. The rogue steps back, watching with a calculating gaze as they observe the standoff.)

Rogue: (calm, too calm)
"I'm not trying to stop you, Kian. I'm trying to warn you. The Heart doesn't belong to you. It doesn't belong to anyone. The Lunar Claw is not a prize to be won—it's a weapon, a key to something far worse than you can imagine. You think you're ready for this fight? Think again."

(Kian's gaze sharpens as the rogue's words cut through the tension. His mind races, piecing together the fragments of information that have been swirling in his head. The Heart. The Lunar Claw. The war. Everything is connected, and yet the full picture is still shrouded in darkness. The rogue is right about one thing—Kian isn't ready for this. But that doesn't mean he won't fight.)

Kian: (his voice rising, his resolve hardening)
"I've been ready since the moment I learned what I was. You want to play games, fine. But this ends tonight. I'll find the Claw. And if you stand in my way, you'll regret it."

(In an instant, the thieves spring into action, launching themselves at Kian from all sides. The rogue remains in the background, their eyes gleaming with amusement as the chaos unfolds. Kian fights with all the fury of the wolf inside him, his claws slashing, his fangs sinking into the flesh of one of the attackers. But they are relentless, and as the battle rages on, Kian realizes that his fight is only just beginning.)

(The thieves' gambit is not just about stealing the Claw—it's about survival, about alliances, and about power. Kian knows that the real war has only just begun, and that the battle for the Lunar Claw is far from over. But one thing is certain: he will not back down. He will not let the Claw fall into the wrong hands—not now, not ever.)

(And as the final blow lands, Kian realizes something: the Heart may have called to him, but it is he who must choose how to wield its power.)

**Fourteen**

# The Forbidden Rite

Scene: The cavern stretches endlessly before Kian, its dark, smooth walls glittering with traces of long-forgotten magic. The scent of ancient incense lingers in the air, mixed with the earthy scent of damp stone. There is no light here, save for the pale glow of the moon filtering through the cracks above. The ritual site lies ahead, an altar shrouded in shadow and mystery, surrounded by the ruins of a time before even the werewolves' ancestors walked the earth. Kian's pulse quickens, his breath shallow with the weight of what lies ahead.

(Kian stands at the mouth of the cavern, every instinct screaming at him to turn back. The air is thick with power, heavy and oppressive, and the ground beneath his feet seems to hum with energy. He knows the stories—the warnings passed down through the generations. The Forbidden Rite is not something to be trifled with. It is a path that leads only to madness, corruption, and death. But he has no choice. If he is to stop the rise of the Heart's power, if he is to defeat those who would use it to destroy everything he holds dear, he must understand the Rite. He must face it head-on.)

(A low growl rumbles from the shadows, and Kian's eyes snap to the source of the sound. Two glowing eyes pierce the darkness, watching him intently. The figure steps forward, revealing itself as a creature older than any Kian has ever seen. Its form is hulking, its fur silvered and matted with age, its eyes ancient with wisdom—and with malice.)

Ancient Guardian: (its voice gravelly and deep, filled with centuries of sorrow)
"You should not be here, young wolf. The Rite is not meant for your kind. It is forbidden—no, cursed. The power you seek will destroy you, just as it has destroyed those before you."

(Kian stands tall, refusing to be cowed by the creature's imposing presence. The Guardian's words sink deep into his heart, but they are not enough to make him turn away. He has come too far to stop now.)

Kian: (his voice steady, filled with resolve)
"I didn't come here for wisdom, old one. I came for answers. The Heart is rising, and I must understand how to stop it before it consumes everything. Tell me what you know of the Forbidden Rite."

(The Guardian tilts its head, as if studying Kian with newfound

## The Forbidden Rite

interest. It remains silent for a long moment, the weight of its gaze unrelenting.)

Ancient Guardian: (its voice softer now, tinged with something like regret)
"Very well. You are not the first to seek the Rite. But you may be the last. Long ago, the Rite was a tool of power—of control. It was not meant to be used by wolves, nor by any creature bound by flesh. It was meant for those who sought to transcend their limits, to bend the very fabric of existence to their will. But they paid the price. The Rite is a curse. To invoke it is to invite madness, to allow darkness to take root within your very soul."

Kian: (his jaw clenched, eyes narrowed with determination)
"I don't care about the cost. If I don't stop this now, there will be nothing left to save. I've made my choice."

(The Guardian sighs, a sound that seems to echo through the cavern, resonating with the very stone.)

Ancient Guardian: (its voice heavy with sorrow)
"Then you must understand the Rite. It is not simply an invocation. It is a binding—a bond with the ancient forces of the earth, the spirits of the land that sleep beneath the surface. To awaken them is to call upon powers beyond your control. It will consume you, Kian, as it has consumed all those who have attempted the Rite before you."

(Kian remains silent, his fists clenched at his sides. The fear in the Guardian's voice only steels his resolve. He cannot turn back. He cannot afford to.)

Kian: (with finality, his voice low but fierce)
"Tell me what I need to know."

(The Guardian studies him for a long moment, then steps aside, gesturing to the altar in the center of the cavern. It is a massive structure, built of ancient stone and covered in runes Kian cannot decipher. A dark energy emanates from it, swirling around the altar like a living thing, the power of the Rite alive in the air.)

Ancient Guardian: (softly, as if speaking to itself)
"You are determined. But know this: once you begin the Rite, there is no turning back. The power you seek will not be tamed. It will consume you, body and soul. You will become a slave to the forces you seek to control."

(Kian steps toward the altar, his heart hammering in his chest. The air grows colder, the shadows deeper as he approaches. The runes on the altar pulse with a rhythmic, ancient energy, glowing faintly with a sickly light. The Guardian's words echo in his mind, but he silences them. He cannot stop now. He cannot fail.)

Kian: (with a harsh breath, his hand hovering above the altar)
"I'm ready."

(The Guardian gives one final warning, but Kian doesn't hear it. He places his hand on the altar, and the moment he does, the entire cavern seems to shudder. The ground beneath him

## The Forbidden Rite

trembles, and the air grows thick with a power that presses against his chest like an iron weight. The runes on the altar flare to life, their light searing his vision. Kian's heart races as a cold, metallic voice echoes through the cavern, speaking a language older than time itself.)

Voice: (ancient, powerful, and terrifying)
"Who dares invoke the Rite? Who seeks to command the forces of the earth, to bend the laws of nature to their will?"

(Kian's breath catches in his throat as the power of the Rite floods through him. It is like nothing he's ever felt before—a burning, searing energy that fills every fiber of his being. His body trembles, his mind spinning as the force threatens to tear him apart. The voice calls again, demanding an answer.)

Voice: (now more insistent, its tone laced with wrath)
"Answer me, mortal. Who dares to claim this power?"

(Kian's body shakes with the weight of the energy pouring into him, and for a moment, he wonders if he is going to lose himself in the process. His vision blurs, and the edges of his thoughts fray as the Rite takes hold of him. But he forces himself to focus, to center his mind amidst the storm of power.)

Kian: (his voice strained, but filled with unyielding resolve)
"I am Kian of the Shattered Pack. I seek the power of the Rite to stop the Heart from rising. I am ready to face its consequences."

(The cavern goes still, the silence deafening. For a moment, there is nothing but the pounding of Kian's heart in his ears. And then, the Voice speaks once more—this time, not with wrath, but with a twisted sense of approval.)

Voice: (deep, resonant, as if a thousand voices speak in unison)
"Very well, Kian of the Shattered Pack. You seek to control what is beyond your reach. You wish to command the forces of creation and destruction. But know this: once you take this power, it will never leave you. You will carry the weight of the Rite for as long as you live. Are you prepared to sacrifice your soul for the chance to save your people?"

(Kian's mind races, but the answer is clear. There is no choice. There is only the Rite, and the power it promises. He tightens his grip on the altar, summoning every last ounce of will he possesses.)

Kian: (his voice steady, unwavering)
"I am."

(With that, the cavern erupts in a blinding surge of energy. Kian's body convulses as the Rite consumes him, his senses spiraling into a maelstrom of light and darkness. The power floods through his veins, filling him with unimaginable strength—and with a crushing burden. The Voice speaks one final time, its tone heavy with finality.)

Voice: (resounding, final)
"So be it, Kian of the Shattered Pack. The Rite is yours. The power is yours. But remember: the cost is eternal."

## The Forbidden Rite

(The energy dissipates, leaving Kian standing alone at the altar. The cavern is silent once more, the air still heavy with the remnants of the Rite. His body trembles with the power coursing through him, and for the first time, Kian feels the weight of what he has done. The power of the Rite is his—but so is its curse. There is no turning back now.)

## Fifteen

# *Betrayal at Dusk*

Scene: The evening sky hangs heavy with crimson, the last vestiges of sunlight casting long, jagged shadows across the jagged cliffs that surround the abandoned stronghold. The air is thick with the scent of dust and decay. Kian stands at the edge of the precipice, staring down at the forgotten fortress, his mind swirling with thoughts of what's to come. He can feel the power of the Rite thrumming beneath his skin, a constant reminder of the choice he made. The consequences have yet to fully unfold, and something in the pit of his stomach tells him that tonight will bring more than he's prepared for.

(As the wind howls through the ruins, Kian's thoughts drift to the people he's trusted—the pack that's turned its back on him, the allies he thought he could rely on. They've all played their part in the tangled web of lies and deception that's led him here. But as much as he hates to admit it, there is one betrayal he has not yet confronted—the one he can feel lurking in the shadows, just out of reach. The one that will destroy him if he isn't careful.)

(Kian shifts his weight, his claws scraping against the stone as he turns away from the fortress. He needs to gather his strength—there is a battle coming, and he needs to be prepared. But as he moves through the ruins, he hears the sound of footsteps approaching, light and measured, too soft to be the tread of a mere mercenary.)

(A figure emerges from the shadows, their form illuminated by the pale light of the moon. It is Seraphine, the one woman he thought he could trust above all others. Her eyes gleam with a coldness that sends a chill down Kian's spine. She is dressed in dark leather, her hair pulled back into a tight braid, her expression unreadable.)

Kian: (his voice steady, though there's a hint of tension beneath the surface)
   "Seraphine. What are you doing here? I thought we agreed to wait for the others."

(Seraphine steps forward, her movements graceful, but there's a coldness to her that makes Kian's heart skip a beat. He doesn't trust her, not anymore. The power of the Rite is a heavy burden, and he's beginning to feel its pull, its temptation. He wonders if it has already begun to change him.)

Seraphine: (her voice smooth, almost too smooth)

"We agreed, yes. But things have changed, Kian. You've changed. You think you're the only one who can bear the weight of this power, but you're wrong. There are forces at work here that even you can't understand."

(Kian's eyes narrow, his instincts on high alert. He's been betrayed before, and he knows better than to trust anyone without question. The tension between them is palpable, and the air feels charged with the promise of violence.)

Kian: (his voice hard, his gaze sharp as he steps closer to her)
"You came here to stop me, didn't you? To stop me from taking the Claw. From stopping the Heart. You've been working with them all along, haven't you?"

(Seraphine doesn't flinch. Instead, a small, knowing smile curls on her lips. She doesn't deny it, but her eyes flash with something darker, something Kian can't quite place.)

Seraphine: (her voice dripping with venom)
"How predictable. Always the righteous hero, always the lone wolf. You never did understand the bigger picture, Kian. You think the Heart is some evil to be eradicated. You think you can save everyone. But the truth is… you're just another pawn in a game you don't even know how to play."

(Kian's heart races as the words sink in, each one striking like a blow to his chest. He steps back, his mind racing, his blood beginning to boil with the realization of what's happening. Betrayal. It was never about saving anyone—it was about power, about control. He can feel the wolf inside him stir, its primal rage rising, urging him to act.)

Kian: (his voice low, barely a growl, his eyes flashing with fury)
"You think you can just manipulate me? You think you can play me like a fool?"

Seraphine: (unfazed, her gaze unwavering, almost pitying)
"I don't need to manipulate you, Kian. You've already made your choice. You've already sealed your fate. You think you can take the Claw and use it to stop the Heart? The Heart is the Claw, Kian. You're too blind to see that."

(The words hit Kian like a thunderclap. The Heart is the Claw. He staggers back, his mind racing to comprehend what she's saying. All this time, all his searching, all his sacrifices—it was for nothing. The Heart, the artifact he sought to destroy, is the key to everything. It's the source of the power that drives him, and it is now bound to him in ways he can't even begin to understand.)

Kian: (his voice shaking with disbelief and fury, his claws unsheathing as the wolf inside him roars to life)
"Then why didn't you tell me? Why let me walk this path of madness, knowing what was at stake?"

Seraphine: (her eyes glint with something dark, something cruel)
"Because I needed to see it for myself. I needed to see whether you were strong enough to accept your destiny. And now, Kian, I know. You're not. You never were."

(The ground beneath their feet begins to tremble, and Kian can feel the shift in the air. He can feel the power of the Rite within him, surging with the fury of a storm. The wolf's power claws at his mind, urging him to lash out, to end this. But Seraphine doesn't flinch. She simply watches him, her expression one of cold, detached amusement.)

Kian: (his voice like ice, his eyes blazing with anger and betrayal)
"You think you've won? You think you can control me, control the Heart? I've had enough of your games, Seraphine. It ends tonight."

(In an instant, Kian moves, his body shifting with the speed and grace of a predator. He lunges at her, his claws extended, his teeth bared. But Seraphine is ready. She steps aside with a fluid motion, her hand raised to the sky. The air crackles with magic as a shield of dark energy surrounds her, deflecting Kian's attack.)

Seraphine: (her voice cold, distant)
"You still don't get it, do you? This isn't about me, Kian. This is about you. This is about what you've become. The Rite has already taken you. It's already shaping you into something… different."

(Kian staggers back, his breath ragged, his mind spinning as the wolf within him claws at his control. The power of the Rite is overwhelming, and he can feel its pull, its temptation to give in, to let go. But he cannot. Not now.)

Kian: (his voice shaking with fury and desperation, his claws cracking against the stone beneath him)

"I won't let you win. I won't let you control me."

(Seraphine's smile widens, and she steps forward, her hand outstretched as if to caress his cheek. Kian's body tenses, ready to strike. But as she touches him, a wave of dark energy surges through him, and his vision blurs. His mind is flooded with images—of the Heart, of the Lunar Claw, of everything he's fought for—all twisted, all corrupted.)

Seraphine: (her voice a whisper, filled with venom)

"You already lost, Kian. You always were too blind to see the truth. Now, the Heart will consume you, just as it has consumed me."

(Kian gasps as the truth hits him like a physical blow. Seraphine's betrayal was not just of him—it was of everything they fought for. She has been using him all along, manipulating him into a position where he would unknowingly serve the Heart's will. The Rite was never about saving anyone. It was about power, and Seraphine is its willing servant.)

(In that moment, Kian realizes the full scope of the game he's been caught in. The Heart's influence has already reached deeper into him than he could ever have imagined. He is not just a pawn—he is part of a larger, more dangerous plan, one that threatens to engulf everything he holds dear.)

(With a roar of fury, Kian summons all the power of the Rite, the wolf within him surging to the forefront. The ground cracks beneath him as his body grows, shifting into something monstrous, something primal. Seraphine steps back, her eyes widening in momentary shock.)

Seraphine: (her voice trembling slightly now, but she stands her ground)
"Then face it, Kian. Face what you've become."

(The night air is thick with tension as the two of them stand in the heart of the ruin, their battle imminent. Betrayed, furious, and determined, Kian knows there is no turning back. This is the beginning of something far darker than he could have ever anticipated. The battle for the Heart, for the Claw, for the fate of everything he's ever known—is about to begin.)

**Sixteen**

# The Gathering Storm

Scene: The full moon hangs high in the sky, casting an eerie, silvery glow over the dense forest. The wind howls through the treetops, a prelude to the storm brewing on the horizon. The atmosphere is thick with anticipation, the air heavy with an energy that seems to hum with the promise of chaos. Kian stands on the edge of the forest, his eyes scanning the trees, his senses sharp, his heart pounding in his chest. His transformation is nearly complete, the power of the Rite coursing through him like wildfire, the wolf's presence ever more insistent. The battle with Seraphine has left him scarred, both physically and mentally, but the true test is yet to come.

(As Kian moves deeper into the woods, the weight of his decisions presses heavily on him. The Rite has bound him, changed him, and now he feels its influence in every fiber of his being. The power is intoxicating, seductive, and dangerous. He knows he is no longer the person he once was. But he cannot allow that to stop him—not when the stakes are so high.)

(The night feels alive, alive with something darker than the moon itself, something that's been stirring beneath the surface for years, waiting for the right moment to strike. Kian can feel it. The air is crackling with energy, a storm on the verge of breaking, and he knows that the first raindrop will be a harbinger of something far worse.)

(Suddenly, the sound of rustling in the underbrush breaks the silence, followed by the unmistakable scent of wolf. Kian's muscles tense, his senses sharpen, and within moments, a group of figures emerge from the shadows—wolves, but not just any wolves. These are the ones who follow him. The Shattered Pack, his pack, the only family he has left. They move with purpose, their eyes reflecting the same determination Kian feels deep within himself.)

Kian: (his voice low, cautious)
 "You found me."

(The leader of the pack, Garreth, steps forward. His thick fur bristles in the moonlight, his eyes dark with the weight of the impending conflict. The others follow suit, their expressions grim. They know what's coming, and they know that Kian has become something far beyond what they ever imagined.)

Garreth: (his voice steady but laced with concern)
 "You think we'd let you face this alone, Kian? After everything

we've been through, you're still our leader, our brother. We stand with you."

(Kian's gaze flickers over his pack, the ones who've fought beside him through countless battles. His heart swells with gratitude, but also with guilt. He knows the truth now. The Rite, the Heart—it's not just about stopping some enemy. It's about something much larger, something far more dangerous. He can feel the pressure building inside him, the storm growing larger with every passing second. It's coming. And when it hits, no one will be safe.)

Kian: (his voice strained, his words heavy with the burden of what he knows)
"I didn't want you to be involved in this. You should go. Get as far away from here as you can."

Garreth: (shaking his head, his voice firm)
"You think we'd abandon you now? You're wrong, Kian. We're not running. Not anymore. You need us, and we need you."

(Kian opens his mouth to protest, but something in Garreth's tone stops him. He knows this battle is no longer just his own. His pack is as much a part of this war as he is, and leaving them behind would be a betrayal of everything they've fought for.)

Kian: (after a long pause, his voice softer, more resigned)
"Then we face it together. But we need to be ready. The Heart is rising, and with it comes the storm we've been avoiding. The power of the Rite is more than I thought, more than I can

control. If we're not careful, we could all fall to it."

(The pack members exchange wary glances, but they stand firm. They've seen Kian change, but they've also seen his strength. They trust him, and they trust that they can survive this. Together.)

Garreth: (nodding firmly)
"We'll fight with you, Kian. Until the very end."

(Before Kian can respond, the ground shakes beneath their feet, the earth trembling as if in response to an unseen force. The air grows heavy, thick with a presence that feels ancient and malevolent. The storm that has been building is no longer just a metaphor—it's real, and it's coming.)

(The wolves snap into position, their bodies low, eyes scanning the trees, ears perked for the slightest sound. The distant rumble of thunder echoes through the forest, and the wind picks up, howling like a pack of wolves on the hunt. Kian can feel the change in the atmosphere, a crackling tension that stirs the very air around them. The battle has begun.)

Kian: (his voice barely a whisper, yet filled with resolve)
"It's here."

(Before anyone can react, a dark figure emerges from the shadows of the trees—a silhouette at first, barely discernible in the dark, but then coming into sharper focus with every passing moment. A tall figure, draped in dark robes, their face hidden behind a hood. The presence is overwhelming, and

## The Gathering Storm

Kian can feel the familiar, malevolent energy radiating off the figure. This is no mere wolf—this is the one who has been pulling the strings from the shadows. The one Kian has been hunting all this time.)

Kian: (his voice hard, a snarl in his throat)
"Reynar."

(The figure steps forward, revealing the face of the traitor—the one who once walked beside him, who once shared in his dreams of a united pack. But now, Reynar is something different. His eyes gleam with a dark power, a power that Kian recognizes all too well.)

Reynar: (his voice smooth, dripping with malice)
"You've come far, Kian. Farther than I ever expected. But I always knew you were too much of a fool to see the truth. The Rite was never about saving anyone. It was about power. And now, it's mine."

(Kian's breath catches in his throat as the words hit him like a punch. Reynar has been behind this all along—behind the betrayal, the manipulation. He has been working with Seraphine, pulling the strings from the shadows, guiding Kian to this moment so that the Rite could be completed, so that Reynar could claim the power of the Heart for himself.)

Kian: (his voice filled with disgust, his claws extending in preparation for the fight to come)
"You think you can control this power? You think you can wield the Heart and the Claw like toys? You're just another

*Lunar Claw*

pawn, Reynar. Another fool who thinks he can bend the world to his will."

Reynar: (smiling coldly, his eyes flashing with a dangerous gleam)
"You think you understand, Kian. You don't. The Heart is not just a tool. It is the very essence of life and death. And I've waited for centuries to wield it. You, Kian, are nothing more than a stepping stone. You always were."

(The wolves of the Shattered Pack growl in unison, their hackles raised, but Kian raises his hand, signaling for them to stand down. This battle is his—and his alone. He can feel the power of the Rite within him, thrumming like a heartbeat, and he knows that if he's to defeat Reynar, he'll have to push himself to the limit.)

Kian: (his voice steady, filled with the coldness of determination)
"Then let's see how long you last with that power. I'll end this tonight, Reynar. No more games, no more lies. You'll pay for what you've done."

(The wind picks up again, howling through the trees, as the two adversaries face each other. Lightning flashes across the sky, illuminating the dark figure of Reynar as he draws a blade, its edge shimmering with an otherworldly glow. Kian's claws lengthen, and the pack tightens around him, their instincts ready for the fight of their lives.)

(The storm is here, and the battle for the Heart, for the future of the pack, and for the world itself, is about to begin.)

## Seventeen

# *Blood Moon Rising*

---

Scene: The forest is alive with the crackling of power, the winds howling through the trees as a violent storm brews overhead. The moon, a deep crimson, hangs like a curse in the sky, its glow casting long shadows across the battleground. Kian stands at the edge of the clearing, his senses heightened, his every nerve strung tight with the anticipation of what's to come. The pack stands behind him, their eyes filled with a quiet resolve, knowing this battle will change everything. The time for talking is over. Now, it is time to fight.

(Kian feels the energy of the Rite surge within him, the power threatening to consume him as the blood-red moon rises higher in the sky. His transformation is nearly complete. The wolf inside him roars with hunger, urging him to unleash the fury within. But Kian has learned control. He will not be ruled by the wolf. Not today. Not when everything is at stake.)

(In front of him stands Reynar, his former ally turned enemy, now clad in dark, ritualistic armor that gleams with the dark energy of the Heart. He stands tall, unyielding, his eyes glowing with a sickly light. His fingers twitch with power, and the air around him hums with the anticipation of destruction.)

Kian: (his voice low, filled with disgust)
"Reynar, you've always been obsessed with power. But you've never understood it. The Heart is not a weapon to be wielded. It is a force that consumes. And you're too weak to control it."

Reynar: (his smile twisted, his voice cold and mocking)
"Control? It's not control I seek, Kian. It's freedom. Freedom from weakness. From the chains that have bound us all. The Rite… the Heart… they are not just tools—they are destiny."

(Kian clenches his fists, his claws scraping against the stone beneath his feet. He can feel the power of the Heart vibrating through the air, its influence spreading like a disease. He knows what Reynar is trying to do—to awaken something ancient, something primal, within him. But Kian is determined. He will not fall for it.)

Kian: (his voice hard, unwavering)
"You think you're the one who gets to decide fate? You're just a puppet, Reynar. You've always been a puppet, pulling at strings you can't even see."

(Reynar's eyes narrow, the crimson glow in them intensifying as his fingers curl into a fist. The wind howls louder, the forest trembling as if in response to the surge of power in the air.)

Reynar: (his voice now filled with a dangerous calm)
"Then we'll see whose strings are being pulled tonight, Kian. I've waited too long for this. The power of the Heart... the power of the Rite... it will be mine."

(With a sudden motion, Reynar raises his hand, and the sky above them crackles with dark energy. A bolt of lightning rips through the clouds, striking the ground with a deafening roar. The air smells of ozone and magic as the very fabric of reality seems to shudder under the weight of the Rite's power.)

(Kian's eyes widen as the power of the Heart pulses in the air around them. It is alive, and it is growing stronger with each passing second. He can feel the pull, the magnetic force that tugs at his soul, urging him to submit. But Kian stands firm, his resolve unshakable. This battle is far from over.)

(The wolves of the Shattered Pack growl low, their bodies tense as they move to form a protective circle around Kian. They know what's at stake, and they know that if Kian falls, they all fall. They are in this together.)

Garreth: (his voice filled with determination, his eyes never leaving Reynar)
"We're with you, Kian. We always have been."

(Kian's gaze flickers over his pack, and for a brief moment, he feels the weight of their loyalty, their faith in him. He can't afford to fail them now. Not when everything is on the line.)

Kian: (his voice steady, resolute)

"Then stand ready. This won't be easy."

(As Kian speaks, the ground beneath them trembles again, this time with a greater force. The earth splits open, cracks forming in the ground as if the very world itself is being torn apart. From the depths of the earth, an ancient, dark power begins to rise, a swirling mass of shadows and energy that seems to warp reality itself.)

(Kian's heart races as he watches the power take form, a monstrous shape coalescing in the darkness. It is the Heart, pulsing with an energy that feels both ancient and all-consuming. The air hums with the force of its presence, and Kian knows that this is what Reynar has been working towards. The Heart, in its full power, is now awake.)

Reynar: (his voice exultant, his arms raised high as if he is the one who controls the storm)
"Look at it, Kian. The Heart is here. And with it, the world will bow to me."

(Kian feels the pull of the Heart, its power beckoning to him, trying to draw him in. The wolf within him stirs, its instincts screaming for him to give in, to embrace the power that Reynar has awakened. But Kian resists, his mind sharp, focused. He will not be swayed. Not now.)

Kian: (his voice filled with fury and defiance)
"You think you can control it? You're a fool. You'll destroy us all."

(Reynar laughs, the sound cold and harsh, like the ringing of a bell signaling doom. He steps forward, the shadows swirling around him, the power of the Heart radiating from his every movement.)

Reynar: (his voice dripping with malice)
"You're too late, Kian. The Heart is already mine. And there's nothing you can do to stop me."

(With a flick of his wrist, Reynar unleashes a wave of dark energy toward Kian, the force of it sending the air around them spinning. Kian ducks, narrowly avoiding the blast, but the shockwave rattles his bones. He feels the power of the Heart trying to tear at him, to force him to submit, but he fights it with everything he has.)

(The wolves of the pack move in, ready to fight, but Kian raises his hand, stopping them. This is his battle. His alone.)

Kian: (his voice filled with raw determination)
"No more tricks, Reynar. If you want this fight, I'll give it to you."

(Kian's body begins to shift, the wolf within him answering the call. His muscles bulge, his form growing larger, more powerful, his claws extending like talons. He feels the power of the Rite coursing through him, but he holds onto his control. He will not let it consume him. Not now.)

Reynar: (his voice filled with twisted delight, his eyes glowing brighter than ever)

"Let's see how long you can resist, Kian. The Rite will break you. Just like it broke me."

(The two stand face to face, their eyes locked, each knowing that this is the moment of truth. There is no turning back. Kian knows that if he falters, if he gives in to the Heart's call, he will lose everything—his pack, his humanity, and the future of the world itself.)

(The wind picks up again, howling like a living thing, and the forest seems to hold its breath as the final battle approaches. Kian stands tall, his heart pounding, his claws bared, ready to fight for everything he believes in. The Blood Moon rises higher in the sky, casting its crimson light over the battlefield, and the storm breaks.)

(The first strike is swift—Reynar lunges forward, his body moving with unnatural speed, his dark magic crackling around him. Kian meets him head-on, his claws clashing against Reynar's dark blade, the force of their collision sending shockwaves through the air. The ground trembles beneath their feet as the battle rages on, each blow more powerful than the last.)

(But Kian knows that this fight is more than just about strength—it's about will. The Heart may be powerful, but it is not invincible. And Kian will not allow Reynar to destroy everything he's fought for. Not while he still breathes.)

(The battle is only just beginning, and the fate of the world hangs in the balance.)

## Eighteen

# The Heart of Darkness

Scene: The clearing is a battlefield of chaos. Lightning strikes the ground with deafening cracks as the blood-red moon illuminates the night in an eerie glow. The storm rages, thrashing the trees and tearing at the earth as Kian and Reynar clash in a violent frenzy. The power of the Heart, now fully awake, fills the air with an oppressive weight, its dark energy swirling around them like a living thing. Kian's body trembles with the force of the Rite coursing through him, but he holds onto his humanity, refusing to be consumed by the power that threatens to break him.

(Kian's breath comes in ragged gasps as he parries another of Reynar's attacks, narrowly dodging the dark magic that crackles in the air around him. The Heart, pulsing with energy, looms in the distance—its dark, shifting form a constant reminder of the battle that rages not just for control of the Rite,

*The Heart of Darkness*

but for the fate of the world itself. The wolves of the Shattered Pack stand vigilant, circling the battlefield, ready to protect their leader. But Kian knows this fight is his to win or lose.)

Kian: (his voice strained, a growl building in his throat as he blocks Reynar's strike)
"You can't control it, Reynar. The Heart isn't meant for you. It will destroy you—just like it destroyed everything else."

(Reynar laughs, a hollow, cruel sound that echoes across the clearing as he spins away from Kian's strike. He raises his hand, summoning a surge of dark energy that tears through the air, distorting the landscape around them. The power of the Heart writhes beneath his control, feeding into his every movement. He is no longer the man Kian once knew. He is something darker—something unrecognizable.)

Reynar: (his voice dripping with malice)
"You're wrong, Kian. The Heart has already chosen me. It's mine now, and nothing you do can stop it. You're too weak to understand its true power."

(Kian's heart races as he watches Reynar summon another blast of dark magic, the air crackling with the force of it. The wolves leap into action, but Kian holds up a hand to stop them. This is his fight, and he will not allow anyone to interfere. His claws extend, his eyes narrowing as he faces his former ally.)

Kian: (his voice hard, unwavering)
"I understand more than you think. The Heart isn't just about power—it's about balance. You've broken that balance, Reynar.

And now you'll pay the price."

(With a roar, Kian charges forward, his muscles rippling with the surge of the Rite's power. He moves like a blur, dodging Reynar's dark blasts with speed and agility, his claws flashing as they cut through the air. The two warriors clash again, the sound of their blows reverberating through the forest like the tolling of a death knell.)

(But even as Kian fights, he can feel the pull of the Heart in the distance, its dark energy thrumming beneath the surface, beckoning him to submit. The power is overwhelming, and Kian knows that the longer he resists, the harder it will be to keep control.)

(Reynar's voice rings out again, taunting and mocking as he hurls more dark magic at Kian, each blast more powerful than the last.)

Reynar: (his tone cruel, triumphant)
"You still don't get it, do you? You're nothing more than a puppet, just like the rest of them. The Heart has chosen me to lead, to rule, and you will bow to me, Kian. All of you will."

(Kian grits his teeth, his claws scraping against Reynar's blade as they clash once more. His body trembles with the strain of the fight, the Rite's power threatening to consume him from within. The wolf inside him roars with hunger, urging him to give in, but Kian resists. He knows that if he lets the wolf take control, he will lose everything. The battle is more than just about defeating Reynar—it's about holding onto who he is. It's about protecting the pack, protecting the world that is teetering on the edge of destruction.)

(With a sudden, forceful push, Kian knocks Reynar back, sending him stumbling to the ground. Kian stands tall, his chest heaving with exertion, his eyes locked on Reynar's form. The pack watches, waiting for Kian's next move. This is the moment they've been fighting for—the moment when everything can change.)

Kian: (his voice dark with resolve)
"You've already lost, Reynar. The Heart isn't your weapon to command. It's a force of nature—untamable, uncontrollable. It will destroy you, just like it did your soul."

(Reynar's eyes flash with rage as he slowly rises to his feet, his body crackling with dark energy. He lets out a low growl, his lips curling into a snarl as he raises his hand to the sky. The Heart responds, its energy pulsing violently, sending shockwaves through the ground.)

Reynar: (his voice a twisted hiss, filled with rage)
"You think you can stop me? You're nothing. You're just another dog barking at the wind. The Heart will give me everything I've ever wanted. Power. Immortality. Control over all of creation."

(Kian's heart pounds in his chest as he watches Reynar summon the full force of the Heart's power. The sky darkens, the air thick with magic as the ground trembles beneath their feet. The wolves begin to howl, their cries rising in desperation, but

Kian stands firm, his eyes never leaving Reynar. He knows that this is it—the moment of truth.)

Kian: (his voice steady, filled with determination)
"I won't let you. The Heart is not yours to control. It's time to end this."

(With a roar, Kian charges forward again, his body a blur of motion as he moves to strike. But this time, as his claws slash through the air, something happens. A burst of dark energy surges toward him, sending him flying backward, crashing into the ground. The force of the blow rattles his bones, and for a moment, everything goes dark.)

(Kian blinks, his vision swimming as he struggles to rise. The power of the Heart is overwhelming now, more intense than ever before. He feels its presence like a weight pressing down on him, suffocating him. But he refuses to give in. He can't.)

(Through the haze of darkness, Kian sees Reynar standing tall, his form wreathed in the dark energy of the Heart. The air around him crackles with power, the very world seeming to bend and warp in response to Reynar's will. The Heart, now fully awakened, pulses with an eerie, unholy rhythm.)

Reynar: (his voice low and ominous, filled with madness)
"Do you feel it, Kian? The power of the Heart coursing through me? It is everything. It is life and death. And I will rule over it all."

(Kian's breath comes in ragged gasps as he pushes himself to his

*The Heart of Darkness*

feet. The pull of the Heart is stronger now, the magic almost unbearable. He can feel it eating away at his resolve, whispering dark promises in his ear. But Kian knows what he must do.)

(He raises his hand, summoning the last of his strength, the last of his will, as the power of the Rite surges through him. The wind picks up again, howling like a living thing as Kian takes a deep breath and releases it in a roar of defiance.)

Kian: (his voice filled with fury and power)
   "You won't break me, Reynar. Not now, not ever. The Heart may be powerful, but it is not your god. And I will not bow to it."

(With a final, desperate push, Kian unleashes the full force of the Rite, his body transforming into a blur of motion as he charges forward. The two clash one final time, the sound of their battle echoing across the clearing as the Heart pulses with dark energy. Lightning crackles overhead, and the storm grows fiercer, its fury a reflection of the battle below.)

(Kian can feel it now—the final surge of power, the final blow. This is the moment. And as he strikes, he knows that whatever happens, the world will never be the same again.)

## Nineteen

# *The Last Shifter*

~~~

Scene: The forest stands still under the weight of the Blood Moon. The once vibrant trees now seem mere silhouettes, their branches twisted and gnarled as if they too feel the tension that pulses through the very air. The storm has passed, leaving behind a chilling silence. The echoes of the battle still hang in the air, but now, the forest is eerily quiet. Kian stands at the center of the clearing, bloodied and bruised, his breath shallow. The Heart, its dark energy now subdued, pulses faintly in the distance, still alive but no longer the monstrous presence it once was. And yet, something feels… wrong.

(Kian's eyes flicker toward the horizon, where the last remnants of the storm clouds are dissipating, revealing the crimson moon in all its haunting beauty. His muscles ache, his body betraying the toll of the battle he fought and the power he resisted. Yet, there's a lingering sensation in his chest, a feeling that something is missing. The weight of the moment presses on him—the weight of what he's just lost, what he's had to sacrifice.)

(Behind him, the pack stands, watching him closely. Their faces are a mix of relief and uncertainty. They, too, are still catching their breath, their bodies tense, but they are alive. They are free—for now.)

Kian: (his voice low, strained, but resolute as he turns to face his pack)
"It's over. For now."

(His eyes scan the group, lingering on each of them as if searching for something he cannot find. They are his pack. His family. And yet, in this moment, Kian feels something gnawing at the edges of his soul—a question, an uncertainty he can't shake. He turns back to the Heart, the remnants of its dark energy still swirling around its now dormant form. What price had he paid for this victory?)

(Garreth steps forward, his face solemn, yet filled with gratitude.)

Garreth: (his voice rough from the battle)
"You did it, Kian. We did it. The Heart is contained. Reynar... he's gone."

(Kian nods silently, his gaze never leaving the place where Reynar had fallen, his body lifeless. But even as he nods, he feels the hollow ache in his chest. He feels no relief, no sense of triumph. Instead, all he feels is emptiness.)

Kian: (quietly, almost to himself)
"But at what cost?"

(The pack falls silent, the weight of Kian's words hanging heavily in the air. They all know the truth. The battle was won, but at what cost to Kian? The Heart had nearly consumed him. The Rite had almost taken him over completely. And Reynar—Kian's former friend—was lost, twisted by the same power they had all fought against.)

Lyra: (her voice soft, filled with concern)
"Kian, you did what needed to be done. You saved us. You saved the world."

(But Kian does not respond immediately. His mind is elsewhere, caught in the storm of his own thoughts. There's a silence between them, a tension that none of them can shake. The forest seems to hold its breath, waiting for something to happen, waiting for the other shoe to drop. And then, Kian speaks again, his voice steady but heavy with unspoken truths.)

Kian: (his gaze dark, his voice tinged with a quiet grief)
"You don't understand. The Heart… it wasn't just a weapon or a source of power. It was alive, Lyra. It has a mind of its own. And even though I've contained it, I can feel it. It's still there, inside me. Whispering. Waiting."

(The pack shifts uneasily, sensing the weight of his words. They know what the Heart did to Reynar—what it could do to Kian, given the right conditions. The power it offered was seductive, dangerous, and it had almost consumed their leader.)

Lyra: (stepping closer to Kian, her eyes searching his face)
"You've resisted it, Kian. You've fought it. You're still you."

(Kian turns to her, his eyes haunted, filled with a grief and pain that no one can truly understand.)

Kian: (his voice barely above a whisper, full of regret)
"Am I? How much of me is still... me? How much of Kian is left after everything I've done? The Rite... it changed me. It marked me. And now, I don't know if I can ever go back to the way I was before."

(There is a long silence as the weight of his words settles over the pack. They've seen Kian fight, seen him lead them through the darkest of times. But they've never seen him like this—vulnerable, unsure, broken.)

Garreth: (his voice gruff, yet supportive)
"You've always been our leader, Kian. The Heart didn't change that. It doesn't matter what's inside you. What matters is what you do with it. You're not alone in this. We're with you."

(Kian's eyes flicker with a moment of gratitude, but the sorrow in his gaze does not fade. He can't shake the feeling that something deeper is wrong. The battle may have ended, but the war within him is far from over.)

(Suddenly, a low growl echoes from the edge of the clearing, snapping everyone to attention. The wolves tense, their hackles rising, and Kian's body goes still, his senses sharpening. The moment of silence is shattered by the sound of footsteps—heavy, deliberate, and unmistakable.)

(From the shadows steps a figure—a tall, lean man, his movements slow but purposeful. His eyes glow with a cold light, and his features are sharp, almost unnatural. The air around him crackles with dark energy. It is Varek, the last of the Elders, the last of the shifters who had once protected the ancient secrets of the wolves.)

Varek: (his voice low, almost melodic, as he surveys the group)
"Ah, so the little pups have survived, have they? How… unexpected."

(The pack immediately shifts into defensive stances, their eyes locked on Varek. Kian steps forward, his body tense, every muscle ready for a fight. But there is something in Varek's presence that unsettles him—a dark certainty that runs through him like a chill.)

Kian: (his voice cold, filled with suspicion)
"What are you doing here, Varek? You should be long dead by now."

(Varek smiles, a slow, cruel smile that makes the hairs on the back of Kian's neck stand on end.)

Varek: (his voice dripping with venom)

"Dead? No, Kian. Not dead. Not while I still have purpose. You've destroyed the Heart. You've freed the world from its grasp. But what you don't understand is that you've done nothing to stop the real threat. The Heart was merely the beginning."

(Kian's eyes narrow as he steps closer to Varek, his fists clenched.)

Kian: (his voice a low growl)
"Enough with the riddles, Varek. What are you really after?"

(Varek laughs, a sound that is both chilling and derisive.)

Varek: (his smile widening)
"You, Kian. You are the last of the true shifters. The last of our kind. The Heart may be contained, but the power you hold, the blood you carry—it's something far older, far more dangerous. And now, I'm going to take it from you."

(Kian's heart stops for a moment as the realization hits him. This isn't over. Not by a long shot. The darkness that Reynar had unleashed was just one facet of a much greater threat, and Kian, now more than ever, realizes the price he must pay for being the last shifter. His future is no longer his own. It belongs to something darker, something ancient.)

(Varek steps forward, the air around him thick with the power of the old magic, his eyes glowing with a dark hunger that Kian knows all too well. The pack steps forward, ready to protect their leader, but Kian raises his hand to stop them. This battle is his to face alone.)

Kian: (his voice steady, a new resolve hardening in his chest) "If you want me, Varek, you'll have to go through me."

(Varek's eyes gleam, his smile deepening into something far more sinister as he steps forward, the dark energy around him intensifying. The final battle is about to begin, and Kian knows that he is no longer just fighting for his pack. He is fighting for his very soul—and for the future of the shifters themselves.)

(And so, the last shifter stands alone in the clearing, his destiny unfolding before him, as the darkness closes in.)

## Twenty

## *Into the Abyss*

Scene: The moon hangs high, blood-red, its eerie glow illuminating the vast expanse of the forest. The wind whispers through the trees, and the night feels alive with a foreboding pulse. The pack is gathered in a tight circle, their eyes fixed on Kian, who stands at the center, his chest heaving with the weight of the choice before him. The darkness grows, thick and palpable, as if the very forest is holding its breath. Kian's fists are clenched, his knuckles white, but the fierce determination in his eyes remains unbroken. Yet, there is an undeniable tremor in his heart—a knowing that the journey ahead will tear him apart.

Kian: (his voice is low but steady, filled with resolve as he turns to his pack)
"I won't ask you to follow me into the abyss. This path, the one I must take—it's mine alone."

(The pack watches him closely, their faces a mixture of fear and admiration. Garreth, standing at the edge of the group, steps forward first. His voice is firm, despite the deep worry in his eyes.)

Garreth: (his tone resolute)
"You don't have to do this alone, Kian. Whatever's waiting for us—whatever Varek has in store—we're in this together. We've always been."

Kian: (his voice softens, tinged with pain)
"You've already given everything for me. For us. I won't drag you into this nightmare any further. I… I don't know what's coming, Garreth. What Varek's trying to unleash—it's beyond anything we've faced. This is something only I can stop."

(The weight of Kian's words hangs in the air. A silence stretches between them, thick with unspoken fear and the knowledge that this could be the end of everything. Lyra steps forward, her gaze unwavering.)

Lyra: (her voice steady but laced with emotion)
"We're a pack, Kian. You're not just our leader. You're our brother. And if you're going into that darkness, then we're coming with you. You don't have to bear this burden alone."

(Kian shakes his head, his eyes flickering with a deep, sorrowful resolve.)

Kian: (his voice barely above a whisper)
"You have no idea what it's like. The abyss Varek speaks

of… It's not just a place. It's a force. A part of me. You don't know what's inside me now. I'm not the same man I was before this war. The Heart, the Rite—it's all a part of me now. And that power… it wants to consume me. I can feel it. It's calling me. It will take me, if I let it."

(The pack stands frozen, their eyes locked on him, understanding the struggle within their leader. They can see the pain in his eyes—the burden of being the last shifter, the weight of the responsibility he carries. But they also see something else: the flickering of fear, the uncertainty of what might happen if he takes this final step into the abyss alone.)

Garreth: (his voice sharp, insistent)
"Kian, listen to me. We've been through hell together. And I know this fight has torn you apart. But you don't have to face it alone. You never have to face anything alone again. We're with you, no matter what."

(There is a pause as Kian looks from one face to another, searching their eyes. The trust, the loyalty, it runs deep between them, but something inside him pulls him back, holds him at the edge of this decision. The power inside him stirs, a growling, hungry force. He takes a deep breath, letting it out slowly.)

Kian: (his voice quiet, but with a new strength that resonates through his words)
"Then come with me. But know this—once we enter that place, once we go into the heart of darkness, there is no turning back. Whatever happens, it will change us. Forever."

*Lunar Claw*

(The pack nods in unison, each member stepping forward, their faces hardened by the knowledge of the danger ahead. With a final glance toward the moon, Kian turns, leading the way as the pack follows, a silent unity among them.)

(They travel deep into the forest, the path growing darker with every step. The trees grow thick and twisted, their branches reaching out like skeletal hands, scratching at the air. The silence of the woods presses in on them, broken only by the sound of their footsteps and the occasional rustling in the underbrush. The oppressive weight of the night seems to push them forward, pulling them toward something—toward the abyss.)

(Hours pass in tense silence, the moon hanging overhead like a silent witness to their journey. Kian leads them, his senses heightened, his body alert to every movement in the shadows. The deeper they go, the colder it becomes, the very air thick with the promise of something malevolent. Finally, they reach the clearing where the ground begins to tremble beneath their feet.)

Lyra: (her voice breaking the silence, a whisper of fear in her tone)
  "Kian... What is this place?"

(The clearing is vast, but there is nothing natural about it. The trees bend away from the center, as though recoiling from something dark and unholy. In the center of the clearing, the earth seems to ripple, the ground shifting as though it's alive. A jagged black rock juts up from the earth, its surface slick and glistening, reflecting the moon's crimson light. Kian stands still, staring at the rock as if it is the very heart of the darkness he's been searching for.)

Kian: (his voice low, filled with dread)
"This is it. The gateway. The place Varek spoke of. The Abyss."

(The pack gathers around him, their eyes scanning the clearing, fear and awe in equal measure. Garreth steps forward, his eyes narrow as he examines the rock.)

Garreth: (his voice tinged with confusion)
"How do we... What do we do now? How do we get through?"

(Kian reaches out, his hand trembling slightly as he approaches the rock. The ground rumbles beneath their feet, and a deep, guttural voice echoes from within the earth, a voice that seems to come from the very stone.)

Voice: (low, ominous)
"Only the worthy may pass."

(A cold, suffocating wind swirls around them, and the pack instinctively falls into defensive stances, their eyes wide with uncertainty. Kian steps forward, his heart pounding in his chest as he feels the power radiating from the Abyss, the pull of something ancient and terrifying.)

Kian: (his voice steady, though the tension in his body is palpable)

"I am the last shifter. I bear the blood of the ancients. I've come to face the darkness."

(The wind howls in response, swirling violently around him, as though testing his words. The voice speaks again, its tone mocking, filled with ancient malice.)

Voice:
"You claim to be the last, but do you understand the price of that blood? The curse it carries? The Abyss does not welcome those who are unworthy. You will be consumed… or you will break."

(Kian's fists clench at his sides, his eyes flashing with a new-found resolve.)

Kian: (his voice fierce)
"I understand. But I will not break. I will not let this power destroy me. I will face whatever comes."

(The ground shakes violently beneath them, the air thickening with pressure, as if the very fabric of reality is stretching, ready to tear. The pack braces themselves, but Kian steps forward once more, determined, ready to face whatever comes next.)

(With a deafening crack, the rock splits open, revealing a dark, swirling vortex within. The abyssal energy spills out like ink, consuming the light, pulling them in. The pack exchanges looks—fear, uncertainty, but a shared determination to face what lies ahead.)

## Into the Abyss

Lyra: (her voice a whisper as she steps forward beside Kian) "We're with you, Kian. No matter what happens."

(Kian turns to look at her, a fleeting smile crossing his face, though his eyes betray the fear he holds deep inside. He steps into the vortex, and the pack follows, one by one, their fates sealed as they descend into the Abyss.)

(And as they enter, the darkness closes in around them, swallowing them whole. There is no turning back now.)

**Twenty-One**

## *The Final Trial*

~~~~~~~~~~~~~~

Scene: The air is thick with an oppressive silence as the pack steps into the Abyss, their surroundings consumed by a void darker than night itself. Kian leads the way, his every step unsure, his heart heavy with the weight of what's to come. The cold seeps into their bones, a biting chill that feels more like a presence than a temperature. The swirling vortex behind them disappears, and they are left in a hollow silence, the only sound the soft, rhythmic beating of their hearts. The ground beneath their feet is made of a dark, polished stone that seems to stretch endlessly in all directions. It feels as if they are standing on the edge of existence itself.

Kian: (his voice barely a whisper, almost drowned by the oppressive stillness)
"This is it. The heart of it all. The place where it all began… and where it will end."

## The Final Trial

(The pack remains silent, their eyes scanning their surroundings, their senses heightened. They can feel the weight of the moment, the heaviness of their decision to follow Kian into the darkness. But none of them step back. They are here for a reason, and that reason will see them through, no matter the cost.)

(A voice suddenly echoes from the depths of the void, low and guttural, reverberating through the very air around them. It's not a single voice, but many—a chorus of whispers, all speaking in unison. The pack stiffens, the hairs on the back of their necks standing on end.)

Voice: (whispering, the words slow and deliberate)
"The trial begins now. Only those worthy may pass. Fail, and you will remain lost in the shadows for eternity."

(Kian clenches his fists, his jaw tightening. His heart is racing, but his resolve hardens. He steps forward, his voice commanding, filled with the strength of all that he has endured.)

Kian: (loud, firm)
"I'm not here to fail. We've come this far. We'll finish this. Together."

(The whispers fade, and the stone beneath them begins to rumble. A crack appears in the ground, a jagged line splitting through the surface, and from the darkness below, something stirs. The pack instinctively backs together, their eyes wide, muscles tensed for a fight. A low growl emanates from the chasm, deep and foreboding. From the cracks, shadows begin to rise—humanoid shapes, their forms indistinct but unmistakably dangerous. They are not fully human, nor fully beast, but something in between, their eyes glowing with malevolent light.)

Lyra: (her voice tight with fear, but resolute)
"What are these things?"

Garreth: (his voice cold, scanning the shadows)
"Shadows of the past. Trials from the old gods… to test us. To test him."

(Kian's gaze narrows as he steps forward, his stance unwavering. The creatures growl, circling them, their movements erratic and unpredictable. They seem to be waiting for something—waiting for the right moment to strike.)

Kian: (his voice steady, a slight tremor betraying his inner turmoil)
"These are our trials. The path is not an easy one, but it's the only way forward."

(Without warning, one of the shadow figures lunges, its claws slashing through the air with a terrifying speed. Kian reacts instinctively, shifting into his wolf form in an instant. The transformation is swift—fur rippling along his body, eyes glowing with an ethereal light. He meets the creature midair, his teeth sinking into its form with a brutal force. The creature screeches, a noise that sends a chill down the spine of every pack member. The shadow dissipates like smoke, leaving nothing but an eerie silence.)

## The Final Trial

Lyra: (her voice rising in warning)
  "Kian, be careful!"

(Kian growls low, his body still tense, his senses on high alert. He turns, scanning for the next attack. The creatures are regrouping, their numbers swelling. They begin to move in synchrony, converging on the pack from all directions. Their eyes glow brighter now, their mouths filled with jagged, razor-sharp teeth. Kian snarls and shifts, his claws slashing through the air as he drives another shadow figure back. Garreth and Lyra join him, shifting into their own wolf forms, the pack fighting side by side.)

Garreth: (his voice growling through clenched teeth)
  "They're relentless. We can't hold them off forever."

Lyra: (her eyes focused, her movements fluid and swift)
  "We don't need to hold them off forever. We just need to survive long enough."

(Kian's mind races as he fights, his body moving in sync with the rhythm of the battle. Each blow he lands is followed by another, but the creatures keep coming. They aren't just fighting with their claws and teeth—they're fighting with something deeper, something more insidious. A dark energy that seems to feed off of their fear, off their every hesitation.)

(Kian's eyes lock onto the swirling vortex of shadows in the distance. His instincts scream at him to keep pushing forward. He knows the answer lies beyond the battle, beyond these creatures. His pack is strong, but this test, this trial, is not about strength alone. It's about resolve. About breaking the chains of fear that bind them all.)

Kian: (his voice fierce, the battle adrenaline pulsing through his veins)
"Stay focused! We must break through! Keep moving forward!"

(With one last rallying cry, Kian charges forward, his pack following in his wake. They fight their way through the dark mass of shadowy figures, their claws flashing, their teeth bared. Each creature they slay seems to dissolve into the air, fading back into the darkness from which it came. But still, more rise to take their place.)

(Finally, after what feels like an eternity, Kian reaches the center of the swirling shadows. His body is battered and bloodied, his breath ragged, but his resolve is as unyielding as ever. The shadows retreat at his approach, parting like mist before a storm. And there, in the center, lies the final trial—an ancient stone altar, cracked and worn by time. A cold light shines from within, casting eerie reflections on the walls of the void.)

Lyra: (her voice trembling with awe and fear)
"Kian… this is it."

Kian: (his voice barely a whisper, filled with reverence and dread)
"This is where it all ends. Or where it begins."

(He steps forward, his body heavy with exhaustion, but his

## The Final Trial

steps sure. The altar before him seems to pulse with an ancient energy, a force he can feel deep within his bones. He reaches out, his hand trembling as it hovers just above the stone surface. The moment his fingers make contact, the ground beneath them shakes violently, and the shadows writhe in fury.)

Voice: (booming, filled with dark power)
"You dare claim the power of the Abyss? You dare defy the will of the gods?"

(The air grows thick with tension, the darkness pressing in from all sides. The stone beneath Kian's hand begins to glow, and in that moment, he knows: this is the final trial. It will either consume him—or he will claim the power that has haunted his every step.)

Kian: (his voice full of defiance, his eyes burning with an inner fire)
"I don't seek the power of the Abyss. I seek to end it. I will not let it consume me. I will end this nightmare, once and for all."

(The shadows scream in rage, but the light from the altar grows brighter, burning away the darkness around them. Kian's body trembles with the raw power of the trial, but he stands firm, the light wrapping around him like a cloak. The trial is not just about strength. It's about will. And Kian's will is stronger than any darkness that dares to stand in his way.)

(The altar cracks open, revealing a radiant, blinding light. Kian's heart beats in sync with the pulse of the energy. And in that moment, the final trial is complete.)

(The darkness fades, and the ground stops trembling. The pack stands around Kian, their faces filled with a mixture of awe and relief. The trial is over. And the Abyss? It is no longer their enemy.)

(But Kian knows, deep in his heart, that this victory is just the beginning.)

**Twenty-Two**

# *The Shifting Tide*

Scene: The moon hangs low, casting a pale, eerie light over the desolate landscape. A cold wind howls through the ruins, carrying with it the scent of saltwater and something darker—something ancient. Kian stands at the edge of the cliff, staring out into the storm that rages over the ocean below. The waves crash against the rocks, their white foam flashing in the dim light, as if the sea itself is trying to break free from some invisible chain. The air is thick with tension, the atmosphere heavy with the weight of unspoken truths.

(Behind him, the pack gathers, their faces weary, their eyes sharp. Lyra is the first to step forward, her expression unreadable as she watches Kian. Her voice cuts through the wind, low and cautious.)

Lyra: (her voice steady, but with a hint of concern)

"Kian… we've come this far. But something's changed. I can feel it in the air. The tide… it's shifting."

(Kian doesn't turn around. His eyes are fixed on the churning ocean, his jaw clenched in silent contemplation. He can feel it too—the unease, the nagging pull of something that's just out of reach. The victory they fought for, the trial they overcame—it all feels distant now, as if it were someone else's struggle. The real battle, the one that will shape the future of their kind, is far from over.)

Kian: (his voice barely above a whisper, laced with a sense of foreboding)
"The tide isn't just shifting. It's rising."

(A distant howl reaches their ears, a lone, mournful cry that sends a chill down their spines. It's not the howl of a wolf, but something… else. Something older, more primal. The sound is followed by the rhythmic crash of the waves against the shore, as if the ocean itself is answering the call.)

Garreth: (his voice sharp, scanning the horizon with unease)
"What was that? That howl… it's not like anything we've heard before."

Lyra: (her eyes narrowing, her posture tense)
"Not a wolf. A creature of the old world. Something that has been waiting for centuries to rise."

(Kian turns slowly, his gaze locking with Lyra's. The weight of their shared understanding passes between them without words. The calm they've fought for, the peace they've earned, was never meant to last.)

Kian: (his voice low, but firm)
"We need to move. Now."

(The pack moves as one, their senses heightened, their bodies coiled for the fight that seems imminent. They make their way along the cliffside, the wind whipping at their clothes, the salt of the ocean stinging in their nostrils. Each step feels heavier than the last, as if the very earth beneath their feet is dragging them toward something inevitable.)

(The storm clouds above darken, swirling with an unnatural speed, as if the heavens themselves are responding to the call from the depths below. The howl echoes again, louder this time, closer. Kian can feel the power in it—raw, unrestrained, and full of a primal rage that threatens to tear the world apart.)

Lyra: (her voice tight, her grip on her sword firm)
"It's coming."

Garreth: (his eyes scanning the horizon, his voice full of doubt)
"Do you think it's the Lunar Claw? That the artifact has something to do with this?"

Kian: (his voice cold, his eyes narrowing as he senses the source of the howl drawing near)
"I don't know. But whatever it is, it's not the wolves we've been fighting. This is something… darker."

(Suddenly, a shadow moves at the edge of their vision. It's quick, too quick, a blur of motion darting through the trees that line the cliffs. The pack stops dead in their tracks, the tension thick in the air. The silence that follows is deafening, as if the very world is holding its breath.)

(Then, from the darkness of the trees, it emerges—massive, twisted, and impossibly fast. The creature is a grotesque blend of man and beast, its eyes glowing with a fierce, unnatural light. Its body ripples with muscles, black fur covering its frame, but the most disturbing feature is its mouth—jagged, filled with rows of teeth like serrated knives, glistening in the pale moonlight.)

Kian: (his voice a low growl, his eyes flashing with recognition and dread)
"A shifter… but not like any I've seen before."

(The creature moves with terrifying speed, its muscles coiling as it lunges toward them. The pack springs into action, shifting into their wolf forms with practiced precision. Kian leads the charge, his powerful wolf body crashing into the creature with all the force of a storm. But the moment they collide, Kian feels something in the creature's form—it's not the resistance of flesh and bone, but the unnatural weight of magic. Dark magic, twisting the very fabric of reality around it.)

Garreth: (his voice strained as he clashes with the beast, his claws raking across its hide)
"It's no ordinary shifter! There's dark magic inside it… some sort of curse!"

Lyra: (dodging a swipe from the creature, her voice laced with fear)
"We have to stop it before it… before it spreads whatever it's carrying."

(The creature growls, baring its teeth in a vicious snarl, its eyes locked onto Kian. The force of the magic within it pulses, sending shockwaves through the air. Kian is thrown back by the wave of energy, his body crashing into the rocks with a deafening thud. His vision blurs, but through the haze, he can see the creature advancing on him, its movements predatory, relentless.)

Kian: (his voice strained, struggling to push himself up from the ground, his body aching from the impact)
"I'm not finished yet."

(The pack rallies around him, their forms shifting and moving with lightning speed, each one using their unique strengths to hold off the creature. Lyra strikes first, her blade flashing in the moonlight as it cuts through the air, finding its mark on the creature's side. But the wound doesn't bleed. Instead, a black, viscous substance oozes from it, and the creature lets out a blood-curdling scream.)

Lyra: (her voice full of dread, stepping back in disbelief)
"What is that? It's not blood—what are we dealing with?"

Garreth: (his voice low, filled with unease)
"It's a curse. A curse that's been unleashed. And it's not just this creature we're fighting. It's everything that comes with it."

*Lunar Claw*

(Kian's eyes narrow, his mind racing. The pack is struggling to keep the creature contained, but every strike seems to do less and less. The dark magic is warping the creature's form, making it harder to injure, harder to kill.)

Kian: (his voice cold, filled with determination)
"We need to break the source of the magic. It's feeding off something—something more powerful than this creature. We kill it, we kill whatever's binding it."

(The wind picks up, howling louder as the storm intensifies above. The moon's glow dims as the clouds swirl faster, the very sky turning black with a fury that matches the creature's rage. Kian can feel it now—the pull of something much older, much darker, deep within the ocean itself. The tides have shifted, but it's not just the sea. It's the balance of power, the delicate equilibrium that has kept the world in check for centuries. And now, that balance is breaking.)

(With a roar, Kian leaps forward, his claws extending, his fangs bared. He targets the creature's heart, the one place that could end it all. He feels the rush of air as he strikes, and the magic inside the beast recoils, thrashing violently. The pack fights harder, pushing against the creature's thrashing form as it collapses to the ground, its body convulsing in a violent spasm.)

Kian: (his voice low, panting with exertion)
"Now! Strike the heart! End this!"

(Lyra, Garreth, and the others converge on the creature, their weapons striking with deadly precision. The black magic seeps out of its form, pooling around them like tar, threatening to swallow them whole. But with a final, deafening roar, the creature crumbles to dust, its form dissolving into the abyss from which it came.)

(The pack stands in silence, breathing heavily, their eyes scanning the horizon. The storm rages on, the ocean still wild, but the immediate threat has passed. Kian feels the pull of something else—something that's just beginning. The shifting tide is far from over. It's only just begun.)

Kian: (his voice heavy with the weight of what's to come)
"It's not over. The tides have only begun to turn. We need to prepare. There's more out there. And they'll be coming for us."

**Twenty-Three**

# The War Within

Scene: A thick fog has descended upon the landscape, draping the forest in a veil of shadow and uncertainty. The trees loom like dark sentinels, their branches swaying eerily in the night breeze. The pack is scattered through the forest, their senses heightened, but every rustle in the distance sends a ripple of unease through them. Kian stands at the center, the weight of leadership bearing down on him more than ever before. His hand clenches around the Lunar Claw, the artifact that had once held the promise of unity, but now feels like a symbol of something darker.

(Lyra approaches, her steps light but purposeful, her eyes scanning the surroundings with the sharpness of a wolf. She halts before Kian, her expression unreadable, though there is an unmistakable tension in her posture. There is something different about her—a subtle change, a distance in her gaze.)

## The War Within

Lyra: (her voice low, hesitant)
"Kian... something's wrong. I can feel it in the air—something's pulling at the pack. It's like we're... divided. Like we're fighting something we can't see."

Kian: (his gaze shifting to the Lunar Claw, his grip tightening slightly as the artifact seems to hum with a subtle, almost imperceptible energy)
"I know. I've felt it too. The Claw—it's changing us. We're not just fighting the enemy outside anymore... we're fighting something inside. It's in all of us."

(Lyra's eyes widen slightly, her fingers instinctively brushing the hilt of her sword as if the very mention of the artifact has awakened something darker in her. She looks away for a moment, but Kian can see the tension in her shoulders, the way she holds herself—defensive, wary.)

Lyra: (quietly, almost to herself)
"It's... it's like the Claw's power is seeping into our souls, pulling at the darkness inside. Some of us... we're already feeling it. Some of us are starting to change."

(A low growl rumbles in the distance. The sound is a warning, a reminder that they are not alone in these woods. The wolves are still out there, but it's not just the external dangers that threaten them now. The true battle is much closer. It's within. The internal struggle. The war within.)

Kian: (his voice soft, though there's a trace of bitterness in it)
"We all knew the price of power. But this... this is something

worse than I imagined."

(Lyra looks at him, her eyes searching his face for any hint of the wolf within, the leader who had once inspired them all. What she finds there gives her no comfort. Kian looks like a man who has seen too much, a man who feels the weight of the world pressing down on him, suffocating him. There's a darkness in his eyes, one that isn't just the result of the war they're fighting. It's something deeper.)

Lyra: (her voice tinged with concern)
 "You're not alone in this, Kian. We'll fight it together. You've led us through every trial so far. This… this is just another one."

(But even as she says the words, the doubt creeps into her own mind. Her gaze flickers toward the pack, who stand a few paces behind them. Their expressions are unreadable, each of them lost in their own thoughts, their own struggles. It's clear that the Lunar Claw's influence is spreading, infecting them all with a kind of fear that is impossible to shake. The pack isn't just struggling against external enemies—they are fighting themselves. Fighting their own instincts. Their own rage.)

(The air grows heavy with the tension of unspoken words. Kian turns, his steps slow but deliberate, his gaze scanning the darkness that surrounds them. Every step he takes feels like a step toward the unknown. He can feel the weight of the artifact, like a chain dragging him deeper into the abyss of his own fears.)

Kian: (his voice distant, more to himself than to anyone else)

"I should've known better. The Claw… it was never meant for one person. It was meant to be shared, to be wielded by the pack as a whole. But now… it's tearing us apart. The longer we keep it, the more we lose ourselves."

(Lyra steps forward, her expression softening as she watches him, her hand gently resting on his arm.)

Lyra: (her voice calm, yet firm)
"We won't lose ourselves, Kian. We're stronger than that. We've always been stronger together. If we can hold onto each other, if we can keep our bond strong, we can fight this. We can fight whatever is pulling at us."

(Kian closes his eyes for a moment, inhaling deeply, as if to steady himself. The fog seems to close in around them, thick and suffocating, as if the forest itself is closing in, watching, waiting.)

Kian: (his voice rough, betraying the strain he feels)
"I don't know anymore, Lyra. I don't know who I am anymore. The power… it's like a beast inside me, clawing at my soul, whispering things I don't want to hear. Things that make me question everything I've ever believed in."

(The ground beneath them rumbles suddenly, and the howl returns—louder now, closer. But this time, it's not just one howl. There's a chorus of them, rising from the depths of the forest, a sound like the howling of a thousand wolves, all crying out in unison.)

Garreth: (his voice shaking, a hint of fear in his eyes)
"They're here. The others... they've come. But this time, they're not alone."

(The pack tenses, their eyes shifting nervously, their muscles coiling in preparation for battle. But Kian holds up his hand, signaling them to stay still, to wait. He turns back to Lyra, his expression grave.)

Kian: (his voice heavy, a deep sadness settling in)
"This isn't just an external enemy anymore. This is the war within. The true battle isn't out there—it's here, inside us. We've all felt it. The doubt, the anger, the darkness. The Claw... it's magnifying it, pulling it to the surface. If we're not careful, we'll tear each other apart long before the enemy gets to us."

(Lyra stares at him for a long moment, her hand still resting on his arm. The weight of his words settles heavily between them, a stark truth that neither of them can deny.)

Lyra: (her voice firm, unwavering)
"We'll fight it. Together. You're not alone in this, Kian. We won't let you go down that path. We'll fight the darkness together. We'll find a way to break its hold on us."

(Kian looks into her eyes, searching for the reassurance he so desperately needs. But all he finds is the same uncertainty that has taken root in his own heart. He's not sure if they can win this fight—not against an enemy they can't even see, not against the beast that has been awakened inside them all.)

## The War Within

(The howls grow louder, closer still. The air around them seems to vibrate with a palpable energy, like a storm that's about to break. Kian takes a deep breath, his eyes turning once more to the horizon. The battle is coming, but it's not the battle they thought they would face. The true war is the one that rages within their own hearts.)

Kian: (his voice steady now, though there's a hint of finality in it)
"Then let's face it. Together. But we have to be ready. Whatever comes next… it's going to test us all in ways we can't even imagine."

(And with that, the pack moves forward, their eyes filled with resolve, but beneath it, a flicker of fear remains—because they all know the truth now. The war within is the hardest battle of all.)

**Twenty-Four**

# Unity or Ruin

Scene: The moon hangs high, a silver sentinel in the sky, casting a cold light over the clearing. The fog has not lifted, but the air feels charged, crackling with an unseen force. The pack is gathered, silent, their eyes locked on Kian as he stands at the center of their circle. His face is drawn, haunted by the weight of their choices. The Lunar Claw rests in his hand, but it no longer feels like a tool of power—more like a curse. The distance between him and his packmates has never felt greater.

(Lyra, Garreth, and the rest of the pack stand in tense silence. Their eyes flicker from one another to Kian, each of them struggling to hold onto the thread of unity that has kept them together for so long. But it's slipping through their fingers, as if the Claw itself is pulling them apart.)

## Unity or Ruin

Kian: (his voice is quiet, barely a whisper above the wind, but it cuts through the air like a blade)

"We are at the edge. I can feel it. The power of the Claw—it's changing us. It's pushing us to our limits. And if we don't act now, if we don't find a way to wield it together, we'll destroy ourselves. We'll tear each other apart."

(The pack shifts uneasily. Their eyes flick to the Lunar Claw, then to one another. They had all felt the shift in the air—the subtle change that had taken root within them. Each of them was fighting their own darkness, their own battle to maintain control. But now, in the face of what Kian has said, they are forced to confront the truth: the war inside them is not one they can win alone.)

Garreth: (his voice low, edged with a hint of frustration)

"Enough of this. We know what we face. We've been fighting this battle since the moment we found the Claw. We can't just stand here and talk about it. We need to act. We need to take control before it takes us."

Lyra: (stepping forward, her gaze intense as she meets Kian's eyes)

"He's right. We've spent too long on the edge of this abyss, unsure of what to do. But Kian, you've always been our leader. We followed you into every fight, into every danger. Now, we need you to lead us out of this darkness."

(Kian's eyes flicker with uncertainty. The weight of their words presses down on him, but the darkness inside—the pull of the Claw—is stronger. He can feel it, clawing at his soul, urging him to take control, to embrace the power. But there's a part of him that refuses to let go of the pack, refuses to let the darkness consume them all.)

Kian: (his voice strained, filled with a mixture of guilt and determination)

"I never wanted this. I never wanted to carry this burden. But I can't run from it anymore. The Claw—it's a force too powerful to ignore. It has a will of its own, and it's leading us somewhere… somewhere I don't think we're ready for. But I'll be damned if I let it destroy everything we've built."

(The tension in the clearing thickens, as if the very air around them is holding its breath. The pack waits, hanging on his every word, but Kian doesn't speak again. He simply stands there, the weight of the Claw in his hand, its dark power pulsing in his veins.)

Lyra: (her voice gentle, yet firm, as she steps closer to him)

"You're not alone, Kian. We are with you. All of us. We have always been a family, and we will stand together now, no matter the cost."

(For a moment, there's a flicker of hope in Kian's eyes, but it fades quickly. He can feel the weight of his decision bearing down on him. To wield the Claw alone would be to risk everything. But to trust the pack, to give them a piece of that power, is a gamble he's not sure they're ready for. He's not sure he's ready for.)

Kian: (his voice breaking slightly, a flicker of pain crossing his features)

"Every day, I feel it—this darkness inside me. It's growing stronger. If I lose control... if we lose control... we'll destroy everything. I don't know if I can hold it together much longer."

Garreth: (his tone sharp, but filled with concern)

"Then don't. Don't hold it alone. We're your pack. We've always fought together. Let us help you now."

(There is a moment of silence, a quiet tension hanging in the air as Kian looks at each of them, his packmates—his family. He can see the determination in their eyes, the strength they are offering him. It's almost enough to break through the walls he's built around himself, the walls he's constructed to protect them from the dark pull of the Claw. But the temptation, the call of power, is almost overwhelming. His hand trembles around the Claw as it pulses in his grasp, like a living thing.)

Lyra: (her voice soft, a quiet reassurance that cuts through the storm of uncertainty)

"We've always stood together, Kian. The Claw—it's a burden, yes. But it's also a gift. We can share its power. Together, we can use it to protect our pack, to protect the world. We just need to trust one another."

(Kian hesitates, his eyes lingering on the Claw, the artifact that has brought them to this moment of truth. The power within it is undeniable, but so is the bond that ties him to the pack. The question is no longer about the artifact itself—it's about whether they can truly unite and wield it together. Or whether the force of the Claw will break them apart.)

Kian: (his voice low, steady now, with the weight of decision settling over him)
"Alright. We do this together. No more hesitation. No more fear."

(He holds out the Lunar Claw, offering it to Lyra, Garreth, and the others. The pack gathers around him, each of them taking a piece of the power, feeling the weight of the artifact settle into their souls. They close their eyes, centering themselves, feeling the pulse of the Claw, the surge of energy that flows through them all. And in that moment, the world around them seems to pause, as if the very earth is waiting for them to make their move.)

Garreth: (his voice tight with resolve)
"Together. We fight this darkness. We fight it as one."

(The pack nods in unison, their eyes bright with the fire of determination. They have made their choice, and now they must face the consequences. There is no turning back. The moment of unity has come, and with it, the final decision. Will the strength of their bond be enough to control the Claw, to prevent the darkness from consuming them all? Or will the pull of power tear them apart, leaving nothing but ruin in its wake?)

(A sudden, sharp howl breaks the silence—a challenge, a call to battle. From the edge of the clearing, figures emerge from the shadows—dark, twisted shapes, their eyes gleaming with malice. The pack has made their choice, and now the enemy is here to test it. The time for hesitation is over.)

Kian: (his voice ringing with authority, the strength of his pack behind him)

"This is it. We stand together, or we fall. The choice is ours. Unity or ruin."

(And with that, the battle begins. The wolves charge, their primal instincts kicking in, the energy of the Lunar Claw fueling them as they rush toward the enemy, their howls rising in unison—a symbol of their unity. But even as they fight, the question lingers in Kian's mind. Can they truly wield this power together? Or is this the beginning of their end?)

**Twenty-Five**

# The Legacy of the Claw

Scene: The forest is bathed in a cold, ghostly light, the moon hovering like a silent witness to the battle that rages in the heart of the clearing. The wind howls through the trees, carrying with it the scent of blood, of victory, and of something darker still. The pack stands in the aftermath of the fight, the air heavy with the weight of their choices. The Lunar Claw, now pulsing with an otherworldly glow, rests in Kian's hand, but it feels like a burden more than a gift.

(Kian's breathing is ragged, his body bloodied but unbowed. The pack stands around him, their faces etched with exhaustion, but there's a glimmer of triumph in their eyes. The enemy has been defeated, for now, but the true battle still rages inside each of them. The Claw is silent now, but its influence is far from gone.)

Kian: (his voice low, strained from the fight but heavy with the weight of his thoughts)

"We've won... for now. But it's not over. The Claw—it's not finished with us."

(Lyra steps forward, her movements measured, her gaze focused on the artifact in Kian's hand. The others follow, their eyes flicking to the Lunar Claw, but there is no fear in their faces, only a quiet resolve. They have seen the power it holds, and they have made their choice. Together, they will face whatever comes next.)

Lyra: (her voice calm, but with an edge of concern)

"You're right. The fight is never truly over. The Claw... it's more than just a weapon. It's a legacy. And we've just begun to understand what it means."

Garreth: (his voice tight with tension, his hand instinctively brushing the scar on his arm where the Claw's power had touched him during the battle)

"It's not just a legacy, Lyra. It's a curse. Every time we use it, it takes a piece of us. It's pulling us apart, and I can feel it. The darkness is inside me now. Inside all of us."

(Kian looks at Garreth, his eyes dark with understanding. He can see the struggle in his friend's eyes—the same struggle that has taken root in his own heart. The Lunar Claw's power is a double-edged sword. It has saved them, yes, but it has also changed them in ways they don't fully understand. The darkness within them is growing, pulling at their very souls.)

Kian: (his voice heavy with a sense of foreboding)

"It's the legacy of the Claw. The power it gives us… it's not free. It takes. Always. We've seen what it can do in the hands of others. But in our hands… I'm not sure we can control it much longer."

(There's a long silence as the pack looks at each other, the weight of Kian's words sinking in. The moonlight flickers through the branches above them, casting long, wavering shadows on the forest floor. The Claw's glow seems to pulse in time with Kian's heartbeat, its call growing louder, more insistent. They all feel it now—the pull of the artifact, urging them to wield it, to claim its power fully.)

Lyra: (her voice steady, though there's a quiet urgency in her words)

"We can control it. We've always been stronger together. The power of the Claw… it's part of us now. But we need to understand it, to know how to wield it before it consumes us completely."

Garreth: (his voice bitter, almost a growl)

"Understand it? After everything it's already done to us? You heard the howls tonight. Those were not the sounds of wolves. Those were the sounds of something else—something ancient. We're not just fighting an enemy anymore, we're fighting the very thing that gave the Claw its power in the first place. And it's coming for us."

(Kian looks down at the Lunar Claw, his fingers tightening around it as if trying to hold onto something slipping through

## The Legacy of the Claw

his grasp. The weight of Garreth's words hits him hard. The power they've been wielding—no, the power they've been choosing to wield—has a history they do not fully understand. A history that has been lost to time, buried in the shadows of forgotten wars. And now, that history is coming to collect its debt.)

Kian: (his voice tinged with resolve, though there's a flicker of uncertainty in his eyes)

"We don't know everything about the Claw. But we can learn. We must learn. If we don't, then the darkness wins. It's as simple as that."

(He takes a step forward, raising the Claw high in the air. The glow from the artifact intensifies, casting eerie, elongated shadows across the clearing. For a moment, the pack stands in awe, feeling the power radiating from the Claw, and yet, there's something terrifying about it too. The artifact is both a beacon and a warning.)

Lyra: (her voice trembling slightly, though she doesn't let it show)

"What do we do now? Where do we go from here?"

Kian: (his eyes hardening with determination)

"We find out what the Claw wants from us. We uncover its legacy—its true purpose—and we end this before it ends us."

(Garreth steps forward, his eyes narrowed, his voice harsh.)

Garreth:

"How? The Claw is a weapon, Kian. It's a tool of destruction. That's all it's ever been. And now, it's controlling us. The more we use it, the more we lose ourselves."

(Kian turns to face him, his expression unreadable but firm.)

Kian: (his voice low and heavy)
"It's not the Claw that's controlling us. It's us—our choices, our fears. The Claw is powerful, yes. But it's also a reflection of us. We control it… or it controls us."

(There's a tense silence as the pack considers his words. Each of them knows the truth in what Kian is saying. The Claw is a mirror, a reflection of their desires, their weaknesses, and their strength. If they are to survive, they must learn to see it for what it truly is. And in doing so, they must confront their own darkness.)

Lyra: (her voice firm, cutting through the silence)
"We'll need more than just strength to overcome this. We'll need wisdom. We'll need to understand the Claw's origins—what it was meant for, why it was created. Only then can we truly control it."

(Kian looks at her, nodding slowly. The path ahead is unclear, shrouded in uncertainty. But one thing is certain: the power of the Claw will either unite them or destroy them. And they are running out of time.)

Kian: (his voice quiet but resolute)
"Then we start looking for answers. We find out everything

we can. And if it means uncovering the past, if it means facing the truth of what the Claw is... then we do it. No matter the cost."

(A distant howl echoes through the trees, but this time, it's different. It's not a call to battle. It's a reminder—of what's at stake. The legacy of the Claw is more than just a story. It's a living, breathing force, one that will shape their future. And whether they fall or rise will depend on how well they can harness its power.)

Garreth: (his voice barely above a whisper, almost a growl)
"And if we fail?"

Kian: (his gaze hardens as he turns toward Garreth, his voice unwavering)
"Then we fall together. But we won't fail."

(And as they stand there, the weight of their decision settling over them, the true legacy of the Claw begins to reveal itself—not in the power it grants, but in the price it demands. The war they've been fighting is not just for survival. It is a fight for their very souls. And the outcome will determine whether they become the masters of their fate—or the instruments of their own destruction.)

(The pack stands united, but the shadows of the past loom large, and the future remains uncertain. Only one thing is clear: the legacy of the Claw will be written in blood, and whether it's their own or that of their enemies, it will be a story that echoes through the ages.)

www.ingramcontent.com/pod-product-compliance
Lightning Source LLC
LaVergne TN
LVHW010215070526
838199LV00062B/4590